Babylon Religion

How a Babylonian goddess became the Virgin Mary

DAVID W. DANIELS

ILLUSTRATIONS BY JACK CHICK

CHICK
PUBLICATIONS
Ontario, Calif. 91761

For a complete list of distributors near you,
call (909) 987-0771, or visit
www.chick.com

Copyright © 2006 David W. Daniels & Jack T. Chick, LLC

Published by:
CHICK PUBLICATIONS
P. O. Box 3500, Ontario, Calif. 91761-1019 USA
Tel: (909) 987-0771
Fax: (909) 941-8128
Web: www.chick.com
Email: postmaster@chick.com

Printed in the United States of America

Second Printing

ISBN: 978-07589-0631-1

Table of Contents

4   **Contents**

CHAPTER 4
GOD'S PLAN FOR HIS PEOPLE

CHAPTER 5
THE TRUE FULFILLMENT OF THE PROPHECY

CHAPTER 6
FROM NERO TO CONSTANTINE

CHAPTER 7
BABYLON RELIGION—REVIVED!

APPENDIX A

APPENDIX B

YOU MAY REACT LIKE ONE OF <u>THESE</u> EXAMPLES:

THIS IS **SOME** OF WHAT YOU WILL FIND OUT ...

---

[1] Not *ancient* Babylon, but *spiritual* Babylon (Rome—see chapters 4, 6 & 7).

HERE ARE SOME <u>MORE</u> POSSIBLE REACTIONS:

You'll *also* learn who "Virgin Mary" *really* is, and **how & why** <u>Satan</u> turned the *real* queen of Babylon into the images of the "goddess" you see around you today.

Are you ready to be surprised by the truth?

Chapter One:

From Noah to Nimrod

120 years before this, God was **fed up** with sinful man. He knew "every imagination of the thoughts of his heart was **only evil continually.**" So he gave advanced notice of His judgment to a man of God named Noah.[1]

NOW THE CLOCK HAD RUN OUT!

[1] See Genesis 6:1-8.

Every kind of land-dwelling, air-breathing creature went into the ark, carrying in its genes the future of its kind. Noah preached about the Flood and salvation for 120 years,[1] but **only his family wanted to be saved!**
NO ONE CARED ABOUT GOD'S COMING JUDGMENT.

---

[1] See 1 Peter 3:20; 2 Peter 2:5; Hebrews 11:7 and Genesis 7:7.

"For as in the days that were before the flood they were eating and drinking, marrying and giving in marriage, until the day that Noe (Noah) entered into the ark..."[1] No one was aware of what was happening, *until it was too late!* The hand of God came down and...

[1] See Matthew 24:38.

"...the same day were all the fountains of the great deep broken up..." [1] Water burst from above and below. Cities collapsed. Civilization disappeared. **Millions** died.

People ran desperately to higher ground. Others pounded on the ark. **But the waters kept on rising.**

THE GREAT FLOOD WAS <u>ONLY</u> <u>BEGINNING</u>...

---

[1] See Genesis 7:11

The few animals and humans that remained battled for survival at the highest hills. But it was **no use**. EVERYONE ON EARTH PERISHED IN THE FLOOD.

"...and Noah only remained alive, and they that were with him in the ark."[1] **And the storm continued.**

---

[1] See Genesis 7:23

Animals, plants and people were sucked into great whirlpools and deposited in layers of rock and mud.

Then the incredible weight of the water collapsed entire landmasses, forming the oceans we see today.

Earthquakes and tsunamis dug out valleys and canyons, while the earth's crust buckled, creating huge mountains. **The world's surface was completely remade.**

2457 BC   ONE YEAR LATER ...

The ark that had preserved them was abandoned as the animals left to populate the refashioned earth.

Finally Noah, Shem, Ham, Japheth and their wives all went forth to begin a new life, and God blessed them.

Then God commanded:

Be fruitful, and multiply, and replenish[1] the earth. [2]

[1] Replenish means "fill."
[2] See Genesis 9:1

Noah offered a sacrifice of every clean animal to God. And God restored His relationship with mankind.[1]

But the Devil only wanted to <u>break up</u> this happy family.

AND FOR 100 YEARS HE DEVISED A PLAN ...

[1] See Genesis 8:20-22.

Adam told the same stories to **all** his descendants, word for word. And **each son** in his turn passed down **God's words,** in the centuries **before** the **Flood...**

... Until finally it was Lamech's turn.

[1] For the ages of people in those days, see Genesis 5.
[2] See Genesis 3:15.

Lamech passed God's words to Noah and his family.

"… between thy seed and her seed; it shall bruise thy head, and thou shalt bruise his heel."

A Child of Eve shall **crush** the Devil! **Good!**

I wish it were **today**. This world is so **evil**!

All three grandsons heard the words of God. All of them were responsible. But only **one** stood out from the others.

| LAMECH | NOAH | HAM | SHEM | JAPHETH |

Shem was a God-fearing man. God blessed him through Noah:

"Blessed be the LORD God of **Shem**; and **Canaan** (son of **Ham**) shall be his servant ... **Japheth** … shall dwell in the tents of Shem …." [1]

God said of the woman's seed, "… it shall bruise thy head, and thou shalt bruise his heel."

Memorize God's words, Abram, just as **we** did.

Noah was **still alive** to instruct Abraham, his **great-great-great-great -great-great-great great grandson!** [2]

| SHEM | NOAH | ABRAHAM |

BUT HAM'S FAMILY WAS <u>NOT</u> SO GODLY …

[1] See Genesis 9:26-27.
[2] Abram was born about **2166** BC, but Noah lived until **2108** BC, when Abram was **58!** Compare Genesis 9:28-29 with the years till Abram's birth in Genesis 11:10-26.

HAM'S FAMILY SERVED THEIR <u>OWN</u> INTERESTS.

Eventually each son would found an ***un**-godly nation.

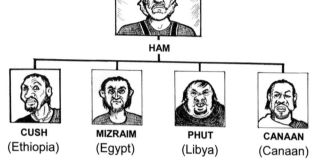

HAM

CUSH   **MIZRAIM**   **PHUT**   **CANAAN**
(Ethiopia)   (Egypt)   (Libya)   (Canaan)

Ham shamed his dad **Noah**, bringing a curse on his youngest son **Canaan**.[1] Then Ham's oldest boy **Cush** bore a son—**Nimrod**. His name means "**let us rebel!**"[2] Guess what kind of kid ***he*** was?

Satan **finally** found a family line he could work through! **These three men** would soon found a **dynasty of evil** that would **create havoc** till the very end of the world:

AT LAST!!

HAM   **CUSH**   **NIMROD**

NOW SATAN'S ATTENTION TURNED TO <u>CUSH</u> ...

---

[1] See Genesis. 9:18-27
[2] See *Unger's Bible Handbook* (1966), p.53 and *Fausset's Bible Dictionary* under "Nimrod."

AS THEY JOURNEYED, THE DEVIL MADE HIS MOVE:

To Cush, *God* was the bad guy, forcing people to scatter across the earth. So **he rebelled** and gathered the people **into one city** on the plain of Shinar.

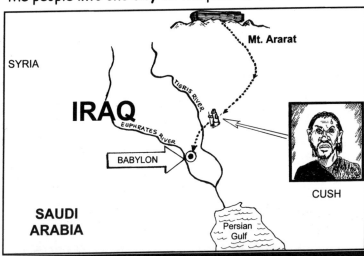

THIS IS THE BEGINNING OF THAT 'GREAT CITY' BABYLON. —SO GUESS WHAT HE BUILT *NEXT?*

They said, "let us **build us** a city **and a tower**, whose top may reach unto heaven; and **let us make us a name, lest we be scattered abroad** upon the face of the whole earth." [1]

You mean he built the **tower of Babel?**

Yes, to **unify** the people under **one religion**.

The Lord knows that in the **final stage of mankind** they will unite in **one religion** to **rebel** against Him. But then His **judgment** will hit.[2] And this *will* happen near the end of the world, **but that time had not yet come.**

So God decided to CONFOUND their language!

[1] See Genesis 11:4.
[2] This is what *will* happen according to the book of Revelation, chapters 13 & 17-18.

You see, up to now people had communicated freely...

Everybody on earth:
- *Thought* the same!
- *Spoke* the same!
- *Wrote* the same![1]

So what did you think? Give me your **honest opinion.**

Well... Cush's boy Nimrod may be big and strong, but he's a **lousy writer!**

Good grief! *I* could spell **better** than *that!*

At **last!** My book is **finished.**

You are so **wise,** Papa!

And **building the tower** had been pretty **easy,** too.

Do you think this frame will **hold?**

Of course. My directions are **very specific.**

Yeah, a *child* could understand them.

Then what is **Uruk's** [2] excuse?

What's the **matter,** kid? Can't you **read?**

HAW! HAW!

For one last moment **every person on earth could understand every other person.** And then it happened...

[1] See Genesis 11:1.
[2] "Uruk" is a fictitious character used for illustrative purposes only.

All of a sudden the builders **had no idea** what **anyone else** was saying! The workers were baffled!

Chaos broke out all over Babylon! If we could <u>translate</u> what everyone said, it might sound like this:

---

[1] Another name for Nimrod.

[2] Just kidding. Actually, teenagers only *seem* to speak a different language!

God literally made it a Tower of "Babble!"

God had spoken in **one language** with Adam. Adam had spoken that *same language* to his many descendants.

Those after the Flood spoke **that language** as well. And God confused the language of those who built the city and tower ... but it says **nothing** about the faithful **followers of Shem**, who did *not* build the city or tower![1] And if Shem's descendants (like Abraham) still spoke Adam's language, and Abraham's language was Hebrew...

THEN THE LANGUAGE OF ADAM MIGHT HAVE BEEN HEBREW, AS WELL!

Now God **used** these different languages to scatter the people all over the earth. It would take them **thousands of years** to finally unite the world **again**.

So God **made the time** necessary to fulfill His promises.[2] Now He would save **millions more** people through history—like **you** and **me**!

These Babylonians were **scared** and **desperate**. They looked all over for someone, **anyone** who could understand their speech.

THEY WANTED TO BE "ONE PEOPLE" AGAIN!

[1] Read Genesis 11:1-9 carefully. Only those that *built the city and tower* are listed.
[2] "The Lord ... is longsuffering to us-ward, not willing that *any* should perish, but that all should come to repentance." — 2 Peter 3:9.

They had almost achieved a One-World Religion.

Then God stopped it. Just like that.

But slowly, cautiously, people started to group together with others they could understand...

First people gathered by families.

Soon they formed small communities.

Eventually they became larger and larger cities. The biggest city of all was still the first: Babylon.

Now *before* they had the chance to form any other cities, they were gathered in Babylon, thinking it would be a good idea to leave the city in their new groups.

BUT OTHERS THOUGHT IT WOULD BE A <u>BETTER</u> IDEA TO PICK SOMEONE TO RULE THEM ALL...

Perhaps it was Cush who made the suggestion. But all at once people thought of Cush's son Nimrod, known as "the mighty hunter before the LORD."[1] He was a big and powerful man.

CUSH

NIMROD

NIMROD WAS *ALREADY* THEIR GREAT DEFENDER!

Wild animals had spread *all over* after the Flood and held the population in terror. But strong **Nimrod** was **fearless** and defended them against the lions.[2]

His **feats of bravery** made him their **champion**. And he *used* his fame to lead and conquer the masses. Though the people <u>no</u> <u>longer</u> <u>had</u> <u>a</u> <u>common</u> <u>language</u>, it was *possible* to group them behind a **powerful leader**.

COULD NIMROD BE THAT LEADER?

[1] See Genesis 10:9
[2] See *Halley's Bible Handbook,* 24th Ed. (1965), p. 82 and 25th Ed. (2000), p. 100. See also the *International Standard Bible Encyclopedia* (ISBE, 1939), Vol. 1, p. 2147 and *Fausset's Bible Dictionary* under "Nimrod" (available in SwordSearcher software). See also *The Two Babylons* by Alexander Hislop (1858), pp. 50-51.

Supporters **scrambled** around, attempting to translate the idea that **Nimrod** *should* be their leader. Many agreed. After all, they *didn't* want to leave their homes and lose the protection of their beloved Babylon.

IT WAS A DECISION THEY WOULD SOON REGRET!

It didn't take *long* for the people to <u>forget</u> God.

The **God of the Universe** was turned into a child's ghost story! But that wasn't all. Nimrod actually **dared** God to destroy the world again!

---

[1] A corruption of YHVH (Jehovah). See "Who Was Nimrod?" by Dr. David Livingston (2003), found online at http://www.ancientdays.net/nimrod.htm.

[2] See Josephus, *Antiquities of the Jews* (1st century AD), Book 1, Chapter 4.

[3] Compare *The Epic of Gilgamesh* (Old Babylonian Version), Tablet III & Genesis 10:8.

[4] Gilgamesh is one of *many* names for Nimrod. You'll find *more* in Chapter 3.

And off he went—or so he led people to believe. The ancient *Epic of Gilgamesh* tells of a great journey, crossing mountains, searching for Huwawa's cedar grove (he lived in "the cedar forest," according to this lie). Finally he returned, carrying "Huwawa" - well, sort of!

> **Behold,** the head of Huwawa! I have slain the mighty Flood monster!

> *Hey ...* that's nothing but some **intestines** shaped into a **face!** [1]

> Hooray! God is dead!

> **Shut up!**

This was **just** the excuse the people needed. With "Huwawa" dead, they *stripped bare* the cedar forests east of Babylon to build sacred temples to Nimrod.[2] He was a hero to his people. So he took advantage of it.

AND NIMROD'S TRUE COLORS BEGAN TO SHOW...

[1] They later made *copies* of "Huwawa's face" of entrails and used them as a guide for *divination!* (They even wrote instructions on the back of them.) See Appendix A.
[2] By 1,000 BC they had *completely wiped out* the cedar forests east of Babylon in the Zagros mountains, so the myths were *rewritten* to say Gilgamesh (Nimrod) went west to the cedars of Lebanon instead to find the grove (and fight Huwawa)!

Nimrod let people do what they wanted *(for a while).*

By now Babylonians thought Nimrod was a pretty nice guy. He got rid of God (so they *thought*) and let them run rampant all over the city. He protected them from wild animals. He even brought the people back together as one nation-city. But they were about to find out an important lesson: **Every sin has its price.**

They would pay for their so-called "freedom!"

YOU SEE, THERE WAS *ONE MAN* WHO WAS <u>MORE</u> WICKED THAN <u>ANYBODY</u> <u>ELSE</u>: *NIMROD!*

The Epic of Gilgamesh records that he wouldn't leave the young women alone—or the boys, either![1]

Nimrod went from respected **leader** to terrible **tyrant** in just **one easy step**. Once people turned from fear of God to fear of man, they were easy to control.[2]

BUT NIMROD WANTED EVEN *MORE...*

[1] *Gilgamesh* Tablet I. See *Myths from Mesopotamia* by Stephanie Dalley (1989), p. 52.
[2] See Josephus, *Antiquities* (1st century AD), Book 1, Chapter 4.

NIMROD WANTED TO BE LOOKED UPON AS A <u>GOD</u>.

Nimrod's image began to be displayed **everywhere**. His power grew as Babylonians looked to him as their leader. *This was the moment Nimrod had waited for!* Once he conquered Babylon, Nimrod took his troops to **other** scattered groups and conquered **their** cities also.[1]

THEN NIMROD REVEALED HIS HATRED FOR SHEM.

[1] See Genesis 10:10. He ruled Babel, Erech (Uruk), Accad and Calneh.
[2] See the *Jerusalem Targum* of 1 Chronicles 1:10 and the *Targum* of Jonathan ben Uzziel. See also *Adam Clarke's Commentary on the Bible* (1810) at Genesis 10:8.

Nimrod used *religion* to control the masses.

Nimrod and his wife Semiramis demanded **human sacrifices**, which were devoured by him and his priests.[1]

WAS THERE <u>NO</u> <u>END</u> TO HIS WICKEDNESS?

[1] See Hislop, *The Two Babylons* (1858), pp. 231-232. Available from Chick Publications. See also Jeremiah 19:5 for similar sacrifices to Baal (Tammuz).

Nimrod had created a **wicked religion**. He turned the eyes and hearts of the people from God to the Devil.

SHEM KNEW NIMROD MUST <u>DIE</u> FOR HIS CRIMES!

Shem came to Babylon and with righteous anger he **sliced** Nimrod into pieces.[1]

Everyone was caught off-guard! The **priests** went into **hiding** and his **false religion** came to a **standstill**.

NIMROD'S EVIL REIGN WAS STOPPED DEAD IN ITS TRACKS ... *FOR NOW*.

[1] See Hislop, *The Two Babylons* (1858), pp. 63-64.

2457 BC

In the days of **Noah** God judged the earth and sent a worldwide flood.

After that God started again with **only 8 people** and **a ship of animals** to populate the planet.

100 years later they had *not* spread across the earth, as God commanded. These *rebellious people* instead settled in a fertile land and created a city and a tower to *unite* the people.

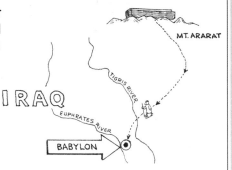

MT. ARARAT

TIGRIS RIVER

IRAQ

EUPHRATES RIVER

BABYLON

So God <u>divided</u> <u>their</u> <u>languages</u>, forcing them to split up into communities and towns. Then **Nimrod** arose as the <u>first world leader</u>, to regroup the people into a single world order, united against God.

And Nimrod was an evil dictator.

So Noah's righteous son **Shem** slew Nimrod. Then the evil, false religion of Babylon <u>ceased</u> … *or so it seemed.*

Actually, Babylon Religion was *just getting started!*

Chapter 2:

Satan's Plan for Semiramis

Semiramis put on a <u>great</u> <u>act</u> for the people.

But Semiramis had a **big problem**: her society no longer had a **leader!** To regain control of the people she needed to mold their **religion**. She met with her priests:

As was the custom, Semiramis mourned for her husband many days. But soon she started messing around with **other men** ... **till the *unexpected* happened!**

---

[1] See Hislop, *The Two Babylons* (1858), p. 62

THE GOSSIP SPREAD LIKE WILDFIRE!

People had mixed reactions to rumors of Semiramis' pregnancy. She was viewed *both* as a harlot *and* as a "virgin queen."[1] For a while things seemed desperate.

And she found it—right in the pages of holy scripture, quoted from father to son from Adam on down.

SUDDENLY HER CHILD WOULD SEEM "HOLY" ...

[1] See Appendix A for more information on this.

God's prophecy about Eve was still in everyone's minds—it had not been **that long** since the **Flood!**

AND <u>GUESS</u> <u>WHO</u> WAS GUIDING HER THE WHOLE TIME?

> You have **no idea** how **big** this thing will get ... Before long the whole **world** will worship **you!**

> Stick with me, Semiramis, and I'll make you the **Queen of heaven!**

> **Anything** you **say, Master.**

This was literally **an offer she couldn't refuse.** In the eyes of the people she would be a "new Eve," whose child would bruise the serpent's (i.e., Satan's) head.[1]

But surprise! She really ***served Satan!*** The Devil offered her almost unlimited power—and she took it! Satan's carefully planned lies would make her *seem* to be, **not** a **pregnant harlot,** but a **holy mother.**

YOU WON'T <u>BELIEVE</u> HOW SHE PULLED IT OFF!

---

[1] See Hislop, *The Two Babylons* (1858), pp. 58-60, 75-77, 244, 277 & 323. Available from Chick Publications.

But it wasn't enough to parade the baby around. Semiramis had to come up with **a story so amazing** that no one would **dare** say the baby was anyone **but** Nimrod!

THE <u>DEVIL</u> <u>HIMSELF</u> MUST HAVE BEEN PROUD!

They started telling the **lie** that **Nimrod's soul** had "**migrated**" from his dead body into Semiramis' womb, so **the baby was supposedly Nimrod—**and **a god**, too!

It's a **miracle, Father!**

And **that** would make her...... **a GODDESS!!**

Nimrod →   ← Semiramis

So in the **next** generations[1], **Semiramis** became the focus of their religion, *not Nimrod—or her son.*

AND IT'S <u>STILL</u> TRUE TO THIS DAY!

---

[1] The days of her great-grandson Arioch or Arius. See *The Two Babylons*, pp. 69-70.

Semiramis and her baby Nimrod (or **"Tammuz"** - which means "faithful son" [1]) had **nowhere near** the power that her husband **Nimrod** had displayed. **They** couldn't protect the people from wild beasts—or even rival cities! Semiramis needed *another* way to **control** the Babylonians. The only way to do this was to **seal them in, building towers and walls** around Babylon.[2]

Now she and her baby (who was supposedly "Nimrod" reincarnated) could rule over the people more completely. But that wasn't enough for the Devil and Semiramis. She wanted to control their **very thoughts, as well.**

SEMIRAMIS NEEDED *SOMEONE* TO BECOME HER EYES AND EARS AROUND BABYLON...

[1] Tammuz is another spelling of *Dumuzi* (or *Dumuzid*), which means "faithful son." See *Myths from Mesopotamia*, by Stephanie Dalley (2000), p. 320 & *A Dictionary of Non-Christian Religions*, by Geoffrey Parrinder (1971), p. 273.
[2] See Hislop, *The Two Babylons* (1858), pp. 30-31.

SO QUEEN SEMIRAMIS INVENTED ...
HER OWN <u>PRIESTHOOD</u>! [1]

THEN AN ORDINARY EVENT GAVE SEMIRAMIS
A <u>SNEAKY</u> WAY TO CONTROL THE PEOPLE...

[1] See Hislop, *The Two Babylons* (1858), pp. 219-24.

I have a **terrible secret**, Holy One. And you're the **only** one I can **trust** to tell it to.

Not here! Let's find a place where we can talk **privately**.

She believed her priest was a "holy man," so she **trusted him** to **keep her secret**. She never even considered that *someone else* could be listening in...

It's my **husband** … He's involved in an **evil plot** —

Go ahead … I'm **listening**.

Hmm... That gives me an **idea!**

All the priests in Babylon served **only** Semiramis, so she got them to **take note** of every little thing they heard during their "holy duties" …

I want to know **everything** she told you.

Of **course**, my Queen!

AT LAST A SYSTEM BEGAN TO TAKE SHAPE ...

As my **holy priesthood**, you will **encourage** people to tell you their secrets. **Find out** all that is **going on** in the city.

Let them **open their hearts** to you.

I'll be like a **father** to them.

What a **great idea!**

Confessional booths[1] started popping up around Babylon.

Bless you, my child.

I've done something I'm **ashamed** to tell **anyone** about.

You may tell **me** ... **just** between **us.**

Alright, **Father.**

It really works! I know **everything** going on ... **everywhere!**

Their **confessions** can make me **powerful.**

Heh! Heh!

This will play a **great part** in our **religion.**

THE NEW "MYSTERY" RELIGION WAS ABOUT TO BE BORN IN A SMELLY, DARK TEMPLE...

---

[1] See Hislop, *The Two Babylons* (1858), pp. 9-10 & 12-21.

Watch as Uruk[1] is initiated into "Mystery Babylon" ...

---

[1] Note: "Uruk" is a fictitious character.

[2] To dull the mind, making it easier to fool him. *See The Two Babylons,* pp. 4-5.

HERE ARE THE SUPPOSED "MIRACLES" :

NEXT MORNING

* **NOTE:**
By blindfolding the initiate and leading him, he is **forcing** Uruk to **trust him**. This is a **dangerous practice. Avoid secret "initiations" like the plague!**

The gold leaf mirror is set to reflect the sun. Then...

Sunlight flashes through the hole, lighting the chamber.

The men move "Nimrod" into position before the hole...

...And suddenly the dark room is like a **giant camera!**

Like magic, a right side-up **image** of the idol of Nimrod **projects** onto the wall. **It's a very *old* trick,**[1] but it *works!*

Satan **replaced faith in God** with **religion** and **parlor tricks.** Now he had to make a god out of **Tammuz.**

[1] For an ancient, eyewitness account of this trick, see *The Two Babylons*, pp. 67-68.

Tammuz was born into a very *confusing* world. His mother's husband (killed by Shem) was **not** his father. Nimrod was already known by many different names, like **Marduk** and **Gilgamesh**.[1] And Tammuz (Semiramis' son, said to be Nimrod reincarnated), was supposed to be Semiramis' **husband as well as her son!** What a mess!

---

[1] Because God confounded the language, the members of this strange family got even more names. (See Chapter 3.) *Marduk* is just a different spelling of Nimrod. In Hebrew, the root word **MRD** ("to rebel") adds an N at the front. But in Babylonian they added a K at the end. So **N+MRD** became **MRD+K.**

[2] Inanna was a name for Semiramis used by people in Sumer (south of Babylon).

[3] Baal means "lord" or "master" in Hebrew and other *Semitic* (Shem-ite) languages.

[4] See p. 43.

To straighten things out for the people, Tammuz may have had to **marry his mother!** *Can you imagine?*

Ancient and modern writings[1] are clear that Tammuz and Semiramis[2] got married.[3]

Something tugged at the back of Semiramis' mind: Tammuz was growing and would soon reign as king! But the queen now knew something about "absolute power":

SEMIRAMIS WANTED IT *FOR HERSELF!*

---

[1] See Appendix A for a listing of some of these writings and where to find them.

[2] Some of her other ancient names are Inanna, Ishtar, Astarte and Ashtoreth. Many more are in chapter 3.

[3] Often writings use the royal term "consort," instead of "wife" or "husband."

ON TO ASSYRIA!

As "**Asshur**," Tammuz **rode north** and **built four cities**, including **Nineveh**.[1] Semiramis played along, play-acting as his "consort"—one of his "royal wives."

But in reality, she ran the whole show!

TAMMUZ DIDN'T' KNOW IT, BUT ... "MOM" WAS ABOUT TO RUN THE COUNTRY, TOO!

Here's what ancient myths[2] have in common: They all say spirits came to Inanna (Semiramis) to drag her down to hell...

She **refused** to tell them where to find Tammuz, till one day...

---

[1] See Genesis 10:11-12. More about the identity of Asshur is in Chapter 3.
[2] Compare the ancient Cuneiform (wedge-writing) tablets "Dumuzid & Jectin-ana," "Dumuzid & His Sisters" & "Inanna's Descent to the Nether World" (see Appendix A).

Semiramis walked in on her husband/son:

This was **too much** for Inanna to take! She knew she would not **live forever**, but the **last** thing she wanted to do was **share** the kingdom.

But in the ancient myths, the *very next thing she did* was **betray her husband/son Tammuz to the devils!** They dragged him down to hell and brutally tortured him. He pleaded with "the gods" and he escaped—for a time. But he was **caught again.**

NOW LET'S LOOK AT WHAT *REALLY HAPPENED TO* "THE BOY WHO WOULD BE KING" ...

IT WAS TIME TO FINISH OFF TAMMUZ!

In reality, when Semiramis caught her son on the throne, she knew she must **act fast** or **lose the power she gained** from her dead husband Nimrod. And the many stories bear **one striking testimony** about how she did it ... [1]

You *must get rid of him!*

I've got an **idea** ... I'll send him on a **boar hunt**.

Probably that winter, he was <u>killed</u> by a wild boar.

Ahh! *Help* me, Mother!!

Oh, you **silly** Tammuz. You're a **god**... *Help yourself.*

Grrrrrr!

TAMMUZ THE <u>MAN</u> WAS NOW DEAD ... BUT:

[1] For more information, see Appendix A.

TAMMUZ THE _LEGEND_ WAS ABOUT TO BE BORN!

NOW _NOTHING_ WOULD STOP QUEEN SEMIRAMIS!

Semiramis got away with the death of Tammuz.
But who was <u>blamed</u> for it? That's right: *the pig!*

Later, on the 1ˢᵗ day of spring, Semiramis declared:

... And people ***bought it!*** She now saw that her son (and husband) **Tammuz** (or Baal) could be molded into **any shape she wanted!**

Tammuz **didn't** seem to have a lot of **personality**, so ...

SEMIRAMIS <u>GAVE</u> HIM ONE!

---

[1] See Hislop, *The Two Babylons* (1858), pp. 99-100.

IT WAS NOW TIME FOR TAMMUZ
TO HAVE HIS OWN "EXTREME MAKEOVER!!"

This doesn't really show Baal's *inner beauty*. Remake him as the **most gorgeous man ever**.

What — *HIM?* Of course, Your Majesty, but I will have to take a few … er … *liberties...*

By the time they were finished with him, Tammuz ended up looking *nothing like* his real self.

He went from THIS:　　　　to THIS:

Baal (lord or master)

Adonis (from the Hebrew for lord or master)

Now Tammuz was not only a god—he was <u>beautiful</u>. Satan was almost ready to *export* Babylon Religion.

There were a **few more changes** in store. Queen Semiramis used her power to make **final adjustments** so that her "priesthood" would live on after her death.

With all the new priests, priestesses, prostitutes and celibates being added, the queen was able to set up even more temples all over the known world.

SEMIRAMIS WAS A SCHEMER TO THE VERY END.

---

[1] Ishtar is yet *another* name for Semiramis. See Appendix A for more information.
[2] Temples of *Ishtar (*or *Inanna)* engaged in prostitution as a form of "worship." See Appendix A for further details.
[3] A celibate is a person forbidden to marry.

Ancient stories say that Semiramis was the most beautiful woman in the world. An often-quoted passage seems to describe the historical evidence beautifully:

She was beautiful no doubt .... Her form was matchless in symmetry, so that her every gesture, in the saddle or on the throne, was womanly, dignified, and graceful, while each dress she wore, ... seemed that in which she looked her best. ... she possessed more than a man's power of mind and force of will.

A shrewd observer would have detected in those bright eyes, despite their ... loving glance, the genius that can command an army and found an empire ... in the clean-cut jaw and prominence of the beautifully moulded chin, a cold recklessness that could harden on occasion to pitiless cruelty .... [1]

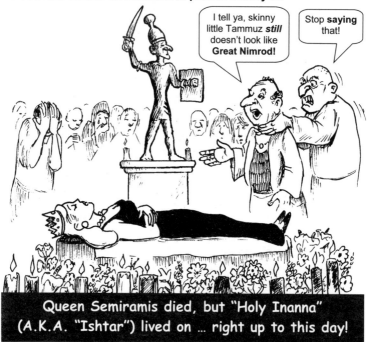

Queen Semiramis died, but "Holy Inanna" (A.K.A. "Ishtar") lived on ... right up to this day!

[1] See the novel written about Semiramis at the *beginning* of modern archaeology by writer G.J. Whyte-Melville, *Sarchedon: A Legend of the Great Queen* (1871), p. 28.

After the death of Nimrod, Semiramis was in mourning—but also in danger! So she quickly took her Babylon Religion *underground.*

But she also became *pregnant!* So Satan helped her devise a way to claim her baby was really Nimrod *reincarnated.* Amazingly, the people <u>bought</u> it.

Everyone believed that her child was the promised "seed" of Eve who would defeat Satan, and thus "bruise the serpent's head" (Genesis 3:15).

Semiramis *used* Tammuz. **She** was the <u>real</u> power behind the throne. Tammuz was a "puppet" king at best.

Remember, Semiramis was <u>married</u> to her *son!* It <u>sounds</u> like she loved her son a little **too** much. But according to ancient writings, she loved ***power*** much more than she loved Tammuz. One day she caught him on "her" throne, and decided she had to *rid* herself of him.

So she let a **wild boar** do her dirty work, then <u>remade</u> her son's image from skinny, wimpy "Baal" into **Adonis**—Mr. Beautiful!

But after **all three** died, Satan remade "Inanna," Nimrod & Baal …

Now find out WHAT they were remade <u>INTO</u>!

Chapter 3:

The Spread of Babylon Religion

SATAN WAS PRETTY PROUD OF HIMSELF.

He had created the first **world religion** to gather the people together against God. He was like a movie director: he had a cast of **5 CHARACTERS** to mold any way he wanted. Notice these **main points** about them:

1. **Cush**—Founder of Babylon (first major city), builder of the Tower of Babel, linked to confusion of languages

2. **Nimrod**—Mighty hunter, first ruler after the Flood, seriously ungodly & immoral, slain by godly Shem

3. **Shem**—Godly man, keeper of God's words, Devil's enemy, the man who cut Nimrod in pieces

4. **Semiramis**—First queen, wife of Nimrod, began Mystery Religion and other cults, bore illegitimate son Tammuz, married him, had him killed, became sole ruler

5. **Tammuz**—Son & husband of Semiramis, ruled with mother, "founded" Assyria, killed by a boar

... AND HE HAD *THOUSANDS* OF PEOPLE READY AND WILLING TO SPREAD HIS LIES!

Satan also knew a couple of <u>very</u> important <u>secrets</u>:

1. WHEN PEOPLE ABANDON GOD'S WORDS, THEY WILL FALL FOR <u>ANYTHING</u>!

It says in **Romans 1:25** that they **"changed the truth of God into a lie**, and worshipped and served the creature more than the Creator, who is blessed for ever. Amen."

But **the words of God** are the **only way** to tell **God's truth** from the **Devil's lies!**

No wonder we have so many religions!

At first the priests **didn't** need to *write down* the "mysteries" they taught. Why should they? They were **making it up** as they went along in the **first** place! So historical fact **de-evolved**[1] into legend and myth:

> ### THE HISTORICAL EVENT
> is typically related to others in the form of
> ### A STORY.
> But a story, *when it is not written down soon after the events happened*, gets <u>exaggerated</u> into
> ### A LEGEND.
> This makes people look better and more important than they are. If this continues, the legend is <u>blown</u> <u>up</u> like a balloon into
> ### A MYTH.
> Suddenly the real people turn into "gods" and are worshipped— usually for selfish reasons, like money or good crops.

Satan noticed another interesting fact about humans ...

[1] De-evolution is the *opposite* of evolution. Things get worse and more disorganized, not better. This is also called "The Second Law of Thermodynamics" or "entropy."

2. PEOPLE GET <u>BORED</u> VERY EASILY!

All things—even worship of false gods, filthy pagan rituals and secret temple rites—all **things get old eventually.** People seek new excitement, new thrills, new mysteries ... even new ways to "godhood." And they are willing to **PAY** to get it!

That's where **old fashioned competition** naturally comes in:

Everyone wants a piece of your worship dollar ...

Archaeologists have found temple after temple scattered all over Mesopotamia. When linguists have examined the writings they contained (if any) the stories of Nimrod, Semiramis and Tammuz are each a little bit <u>different</u> from the others. Why? Because each temple had to have something *different* to offer, to draw in paying customers. **And it's the same today!**

Many people celebrated Semiramis (using the name "Ishtar," among others) on the 1st day of spring, which is either March 20th or 21st. If we count from "Ishtar's Day" (say, March 20th) for the length of the average pregnancy (40 weeks), we come to December 25th, the day celebrated as Tammuz's (the sun god's) birthday![1]

IS *THAT A* <u>COINCIDENCE?</u> —*No way!*

BUT THE DEVIL'S PLAN HAD ONLY BEGUN ...

[1] Some say that December 25th is *not* the sun god's birthday. To find out the truth, see Appendix A.

After a while, Satan **filled** the whole calendar with ceremonies for **Tammuz's birth**, **death**, **rebirth** and for **Semiramis' birthday**, **descent into hell** and **her ascent from hell** and lots of *blending* of them under any of a number of different names.[1] *Whew!* Eventually even the **date of Tammuz's death changed** to match the seasons, the weather or the local traditions of different cities.

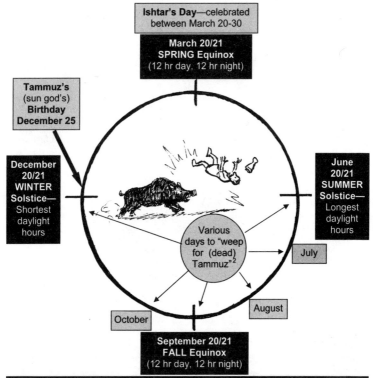

> **Ishtar's Day**—celebrated between March 20-30
>
> **March 20/21 SPRING Equinox** (12 hr day, 12 hr night)
>
> **Tammuz's (sun god's) Birthday December 25**
>
> **December 20/21 WINTER Solstice**— Shortest daylight hours
>
> **June 20/21 SUMMER Solstice**— Longest daylight hours
>
> Various days to "weep for (dead) Tammuz"[2]
>
> July
>
> August
>
> October
>
> **September 20/21 FALL Equinox** (12 hr day, 12 hr night)

The many *different* names given to the *same* "gods" made the pagan calendar even *more* confusing ...

[1] For more information about the pagan calendar, see Appendix A.
[2] These days were accompanied by filthy orgies and debauchery of *every* kind. He was usually "resurrected" a few days after he died (except when he "rose" in Spring).

Remember: **God** divided the language at Babel. So <u>instantly</u> there were maybe **30+ different ways** to say the **exact same word!**[1] So it is not surprising that there were many names for the same **person**, as well.

Each **cult** used certain names for each of the **three main characters**.

Each **language** also picked **one** name for a god over the others.

But all these differences are *nothing* compared to what *Egypt* did to Babylon Religion!

---

[1] Historical linguists make groups of "parent" languages. Take all of them, minus one (Shem's) and you have the number of languages God divided at the Tower of Babel.

Satan decided to send "the gods" through Egypt.

The religion of old Babylon moved west, then south, down to **Egypt**, the land of **big shot priests** and know-it-alls. **Nothing** was good enough for them.

These God-hating priestly "intellectuals" **changed the story** of what had happened in Babylon. They **reworked** the history[1] for the "little people" ...

You know—like Hollywood!

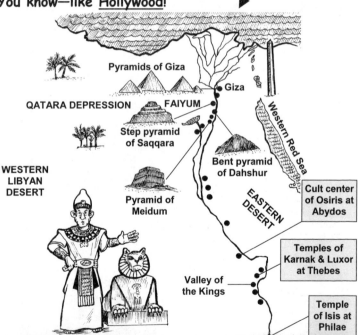

Pyramids of Giza

Giza

QATARA DEPRESSION   **FAIYUM**

Step pyramid of Saqqara

Western Red Sea

Bent pyramid of Dahshur

WESTERN LIBYAN DESERT

Pyramid of Meidum

EASTERN DESERT

Cult center of Osiris at Abydos

Temples of Karnak & Luxor at Thebes

Valley of the Kings

Temple of Isis at Philae

Imagine it <u>as</u> <u>if</u> the Egyptians were casting a movie...

[1] For more information showing how Egypt *rewrote* ancient stories and mythology, see Appendix A. Information for this map from Gahlin, *Egyptian Religion* (2002), p. 6.

After they left the Garden of Eden, Adam & Eve had two sons: **Cain** and **Abel**.[1] **Cain** grew **angry** and jealous of godly Abel and **slew** him.

The death of Abel **instantly** ended the godly line. But God showed mercy and gave Adam and Eve another son: **Seth**.

Of course, Adam and Eve had **many** children **after** Seth, both boys and girls, who grew up, married and had families. But only **Seth** is mentioned. The Bible says Seth grew up and had a son named **Enos**. "... *then* began men to call upon the name of the Lord."[2] So in place of Abel...

SETH WAS NOW THE HEAD OF THE GODLY LINE.

A few generations later **Noah** was born. So the **godly line survived** the worldwide Flood. Then from Seth's line came Jesus—even you and me!

SO WHAT DID THEY *RENAME* SHEM,[3] WHEN THEY CHANGED HIM INTO A BAD GUY? *SETH!!*[4]

---

[1] See Genesis 4:1-12.
[2] See Genesis 4:25-26; 5:1-11.
[3] See *Two Babylons*, p. 65.
[4] Also known as "Set" and "Sutekh" (p. 85).

ON AND ON THE "REVISIONS" WENT...

… What about her little brat kid, **Tammuz … Asshur, Baal, Adonis—whatever?**

We'll call the kid **Horus.** He's our **payback hero**— he goes for **revenge** over his **dad** that **Seth** killed!

REVENGE SELLS! But let's **not** say they're **human.** Let's make them all **gods!**

… And let's call them all **brothers and sisters … except** *Horus*, of course! [1]

Yeah, but will the **people** *buy* all this?

Of course! And you know **why?** Because <u>we are Egypt</u> … and *everyone* listens to what **we** say!

AMEN!

Amen? (What **are** you, kid—a **Shemite?**) [2]

NOW IT WAS TIME TO PICK THE "ACTORS" ...

[1] The priests made Isis, Osiris, Seth & Nephthys the "children" of gods Seb (now also called Geb) & Nut. Horus came from Isis and (dead) Osiris. See Littleton, *Mythology: The Illustrated Anthology of World Myth and Storytelling* (2002), pp. 12, 37 & 50-53.

[2] "Amen" means "truth" or "let it be so" in Hebrew, the language of Shem.

No cast is complete without the right characters.

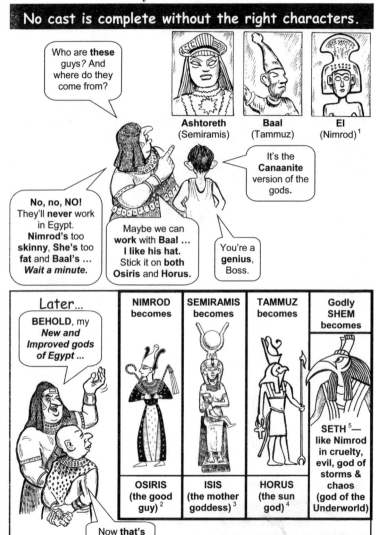

Who are **these** guys? And where do they come from?

Ashtoreth (Semiramis)

Baal (Tammuz)

El (Nimrod) [1]

It's the **Canaanite** version of the gods.

No, no, NO! They'll **never** work in Egypt. **Nimrod's** too **skinny, She's** too **fat** and **Baal's** ... *Wait a minute.*

Maybe we can **work** with **Baal** ... **I like his hat.** Stick it on **both** Osiris and Horus.

You're a **genius**, Boss.

Later...

BEHOLD, my *New and Improved gods* of Egypt ...

NIMROD becomes	SEMIRAMIS becomes	TAMMUZ becomes	Godly SHEM becomes
OSIRIS (the good guy) [2]	**ISIS** (the mother goddess) [3]	**HORUS** (the sun god) [4]	**SETH** [5]— like Nimrod in cruelty, evil, god of storms & chaos (god of the Underworld)

Now **that's** more **like it!**

FINALLY CAME THEIR "PREMIERE" NIGHT ...

[1] See p. 81 & End Note for p. 78.   [3] See pp. 92-93.   [5] See pp. 79 & 85.
[2] See p. 79.   [4] See pp. 89 & 212.

Egypt was largely a desert country, but also a land of massive pomp and ceremony. Somewhere around 2300 BC they showed off their new gods to attract the "beautiful people" (as well as their servants) to their display of: **Babylon Religion, Egypt style:**

From Egypt these fake deities went all over the world. People had a choice: *Their gods or Babylon's.*

TAKE A LOOK AT THE MESS THEY CREATED!

LET'S START WITH NIMROD...

NIMROD

Marduk

In Babylon he was known as **Marduk.**[1] By that name he became the "patron god of Babylon." He is also called by these names: **Amaruduk, Bel-Marduk, Belos, An & Anu** (in Sumeria south of Babylon) **& Merodach.**[2]

Later the cults made Nimrod into the "god of trading," and a teacher and writer. For this they gave him the name, **Nebo.** In Hebrew, "nebo" means "prophet," so Nebo is a god of prophecy, too.[3]

Nebo

But as an immoral, ungodly and tyrant ruler, he is best known as **Gilgamesh,** the mighty hunter.[4]

Notice the lions

Gilgamesh carving found at the palace of Khorsabad in Assyria

NIMROD WAS AN EASY "GOD" TO START WITH...

[1] See p. 51, note #1.
[2] And in the "Hymn of the 50 Names of Marduk" are 49 **more** names given to him!
[3] According to Hislop, Nimrod inherited the names "Nebo" and "Bel" from his dad Cush, who built Babel & the tower. See Hislop, *The Two Babylons*, pp. 25-26, 34.
[4] See pp. 28-31 and other references there.

LATER KINGS WANTED TO *IMITATE* NIMROD!

The 8-pointed star is a symbol of Ishtar.

Naram-Sin conquers the Lullubians

A couple of generations later, the conqueror King **Naram-Sin** had monuments made of himself dressed up like Nimrod. Rulers would adopt Nimrod's style and dress when they wanted to be worshipped as gods!

100 years later, King **Anubanini** copied Naram-Sin and had **himself** made up to be a god, **too**. Only he added the **clear** depiction of **Inanna/Ishtar** helping him to defeat his enemies.

Babylonian rock cut relief of Anubanini (king of the Lullubians) & Ishtar. Found in Sar-i-pul, Afghanistan.

Sargon I, king of Akkad

Ancient writings show that **Sargon I** lived at the **same time** and ruled over the **same lands** as Nimrod. So what's the difference? Sargon was not an *imitator*. It's just **another** name for **Nimrod** himself.[1]

NIMROD KEPT CHANGING YEAR AFTER YEAR ...

[1] Sargon I ruled over Akkad and had his capital as Babylon, just like Biblical Nimrod. See Genesis 10:10. See also *Unger's Bible Handbook* (1966), pp. 53 & 59.

... AND EACH <u>CITY</u> CHANGED HIS IMAGE, TOO!

The Bible says of Nimrod:
"And **the beginning** of his kingdom was **Babel**, and **Erech**, and **Accad**, and **Calneh**, in the land of Shinar."[1]

Nimrod was known by **different names**, even in the most **ancient** cities. Why? Because after Babel, people of different languages gathered into communities. And **Nimrod ruled over** <u>all</u> **of them**.[2]

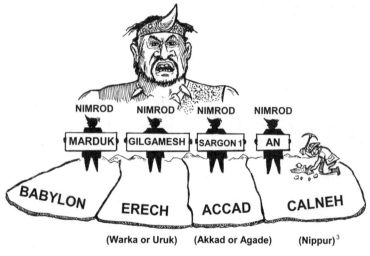

NIMROD   NIMROD   NIMROD   NIMROD

MARDUK   GILGAMESH   SARGON 1   AN

BABYLON   ERECH   ACCAD   CALNEH

(Warka or Uruk)   (Akkad or Agade)   (Nippur)[3]

Nimrod was the **very image of power**. He was **big** and **strong**. He **inspired armies to battle**. But he had his **weak points**, too. He was <u>also</u> an **evil, satanic pervert!** The Egyptians decided to clean him up. But **someone** had to be the bad guy. That's why they chose **Shem**.

So they cleaned up Nimrod, and dirtied down Shem:

[1] Genesis 10:10
[2] See pp. 25-27.
[3] See Appendix A for more information.

Let's summarize how Egypt changed Nimrod ...

They took dirty old ungodly Nimrod ...	Gave him a bath, put him on a diet, dressed him up, then changed his name ...	And presto! Now he's the perfectly good and happy god Osiris! [1]

Now let's review what they did to Shem ...

They took clean and godly Shem ...	Dumped Nimrod's evil and ungodliness on him, then changed his name ...	And presto! Now he's the perfectly wicked and angry god Seth!

So you see how Nimrod was made into a "good" god...

[1] See Appendix A.

Now Nimrod could be made to look LESS VIOLENT!

This picture is highly symbolic. It depicts **Nimrod** as a **god**. Notice how it shows him holding a **spotted fawn**. The fawn is actually a *symbol* of Nimrod himself. So is the branch he is holding, and other things, too![1]

As Roman **Bacchus** and Greek **Dionysius**, Nimrod was the god of wine drinking and revelry. Dionysius was drawn as wearing a *nebris* (fawn skin).[2] But even though he's jolly — and drunk, Bacchus was *fierce* in battle.

As Greek **Pan** and Roman **Faunus**, Nimrod became a musical god of woods and wildlife. Pan was the son of **Hermes** (Roman **Mercury**), another name for **Cush**.[3]

But Nimrod was <u>not</u> all fun and games!

NIMROD WAS <u>SATANIC</u>!

As **Moloch** (or **Molech**), Nimrod demanded *human sacrifices—usually babies!* He's clearly named in the Bible 11 times. ***Read Leviticus 18:21.***

But he became more than that...

---

[1] In the perverted Greek Bible called the "Septuagint" (LXX), it doesn't say "Nimrod." It says "*Nebrod*" (Greek for "spotted fawn")! For more information, see Appendix A.

[2] *Nebris* (Greek for "fawn skin") is another reference to Nimrod.

[3] Cush is Nimrod's dad. See Gen. 10:8 and Hislop, *Two Babylons* (1858), pp. 25-29.

NIMROD BECAME KNOWN AS <u>CHIEF</u> OF "GODS" !

In **Canaan**, Nimrod **looked** mild-mannered as skinny **El**. But this guy was the **head of the gods**. And though *his* name is not mentioned in the Bible, his wife **Ashtoreth (Semiramis)**, is found **9** times, and her son/husband **Baal (Tammuz)** is mentioned no less than **76** times!

As the Greek god **Zeus** (the Roman **Jupiter**) he **wasn't** mild-mannered **at all**. The myths said he had a bad **temper**, hurled **lightning bolts** and bore piles of kids with both goddesses and human women. Zeus actually blends parts of both Nimrod and Tammuz (Baal) together. This sounds confusing, but remember: *almost <u>all</u> the gods were created from only <u>five</u> <u>real</u> <u>people</u>!*

In later myths, **Kronos** (Roman **Saturn**) was added as **Zeus's father.** And Kronos' wife, **Rhea**, the "builder

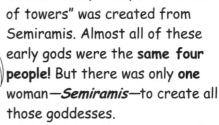

of towers" was created from Semiramis. Almost all of these early gods were the **same four people**! But there was only **one** woman—*Semiramis*—to create all those goddesses.
That lady <u>really</u> gets around!

BUT AS YOU'LL SEE, SEMIRAMIS WAS <u>NO LADY</u>!

ALL GODDESSES WERE MADE FROM _ONE_ _WOMAN_.

Semiramis was a multi-faceted woman. Each aspect of her personality became the starting place for goddess religion. The **most obvious** one is the **GODDESS OF LOVE**. But love takes many forms, and not all of them are good. Semiramis' kind of "love" brought **prostitution** to the world.

SEMIRAMIS

Her most famous forms are **Venus** (Roman) and **Aphrodite** (Greek). Just like Semiramis, Aphrodite had many lovers, and temples to her engaged in prostitution and all forms of debauchery. Other names for her as "love goddess" are **Inanna**, **Ishtar**, **Astarte**, **Ashtoreth** and **Asherah**.

BUT SHE WAS NOT JUST A GODDESS OF "LOVE" ...

SHE WAS ALSO THE GODDESS OF WAR!

Ishtar

From the earliest drawings of her as **Ishtar**, Semiramis was known as a **lady of war**. To kings she was a **warrior goddess**. They **prayed** to her before battle and **honored** her with **statues** and **praises** when they defeated their enemies.

Athena

As a warrior she is best known as **Athena, Minerva, Artemis** and **Diana**. She is most often pictured with a bow.

Artemis

But there is **more** to this picture than meets the eye. Carefully look at the **bow** she is holding. Do you notice the shape?

Diana

That is not an **ordinary** bow. It actually symbolizes the **crescent moon!** And in Diana's bow you can see a **star** as well. *That's no coincidence.* Semiramis is also a moon goddess[1] and goddess of the morning/evening star (the planet Venus).

BUT SATAN MADE SEMIRAMIS EVEN BIGGER ...

[1] See the list in Appendix A.

SEMIRAMIS BECAME LIKE NIMROD HIMSELF!

In this Assyrian drawing of Nimrod, first he kills the bull. Then he takes on some of the bull's attributes—the horns, tail and hooves. Then he goes after the lion. **Later kings wore horns to say they were gods**. (See p. 77.)

As **Ishtar** and **Inanna**, Semiramis got **dressed up** like **Nimrod**—*horns and all!*

As **Cybele** Semiramis was known as the **"builder of cities,"** as well as **"protector"** in time of war.

Inanna dressed like Nimrod, with crescent moon and morning star, riding her "storm dragon."

Semiramis was made into **hundreds of goddesses**, beginning only **one generation** after her death (about 2300 BC). She was a lover, a warrior or a ruler. She was a mother goddess, a sister goddess or a wife goddess. She was associated with the morning/evening star or the moon. **Often she was all of these rolled up into one!**

But Semiramis wasn't done "transforming" yet. She needed to become even **more powerful** and **appeal** to **more people** before she would **entrap the world**.

First, she had to become <u>her own mirror image</u>!

SHE BECAME GODDESS OF THE "*UNDERWORLD*."

Ereshkigal or Lilith, wearing the Sumerian crown and "rod & ring" of royal authority. 2000 BC.

In this form Semiramis had **many names**. First she was **Ereshkigal**, then **Lilitu, Lilu and Lilith**. She was known as the "**queen of the demons**" and the **opposite** of Inanna-Ishtar. (But this idol is *still* sometimes called "**Ishtar**" by **mistake**.)

Once humans are made into gods, they have to be **related** to each other. So the stories made Semiramis' "mirror image" into her **sister**. Egyptians said **Isis** had a **sister** called **Nephthys** who ruled the **underworld**.

Egyptian Isis nursing Horus, and her mirror image Nephthys.

INTERESTING FACT: Since Nephthys needed a **husband** too, who do you think they **made up** to rule the underworld *with* her? **Who else? Godly Shem**, now changed into **evil Seth**, became the "ruler of the dead!" Egyptians later renamed him **Sutekh** (in Greek, the evil **Typhon**)!

Now Semiramis was just <u>one</u> <u>step</u> <u>away</u> from being...

THE GODDESS OF WITCHCRAFT!

As the Greek **Hecate**, Semiramis was more than the goddess of the underworld. She also was believed to rule over the **gateway**, or **"crossroads"** to the realm of the dead. Her idols were found where three roads met. **Dogs** and **black lambs** were **sacrificed** to her. It is clear from the evidence she is **a goddess of black magic & witchcraft!**[1]

Hecate has many other names, such as: **Artemis**, **Athena**, **Dione**, **Melusine**, **Aphrodite**, **Keridwen**, **Dana**, **Arianrhod**, **Isis** and **Brigit!**

The "witch" of the new millennium

Is there *more* evidence for this? You bet!

[1] For this section see the notes and references in Appendix A.

Evidence **proves** pagans **sacrificed humans** to Semiramis, as well as animals. M. Esther Harding wrote:

> The priestess of the moon goddess ... had also to impersonate [the goddess] in her dark and destructive aspect. ... **infant sacrifices** were regularly performed in honor of, certainly, some forms of the goddess. It is recorded, for instance, that **around the sacred stone** which represented the goddess **Astarte, hundreds** of **skeletons** of **human infants** have been found. ... **first-born children** and animals **were sacrificed to** her.[1]

But witchcraft was not confined to *European* gods and goddesses. Let's go over to the Americas ...

[1] M. Esther Harding, *Woman's Mysteries: Ancient & Modern* (1971), p. 138. See also William Schnoebelen's *Wicca: Satan's Little White Lie* (1991), pp. 117-118, available from Chick Publications. For more information, see Appendix A.

She was goddess of witchcraft in the Americas, too!

Tlazolteotl from the detail of a page in the Mesoamerican Borgia Codex (1200-1500).

Tlazolteotl (TLAS-ole-tay-OH-tuhl) was the Aztec **moon goddess** *and* represented the **planet Venus** (just like Ishtar). She was the goddess of **witchcraft** and **the power behind all magic, including "black magic!"** [1]

Tlazolteotl, the witch of the Americas, complete with pointed hat and broom.

NOW DO YOU SEE WHO SHE <u>REALLY</u> IS?

Though this goddess is from **Mexico** and **Central America**, her **symbols** are **identical** to the witches of Europe! Remember, **all gods and goddesses were created from *5 historical people*!**

And history tells us the witch Semiramis had a son ...

[1] For more information, see the notes in Appendix A.

THE BOY OF A THOUSAND FACES!

We already know how **Tammuz**
(or **Dumuzi**) got many of his names:

TAMMUZ

In Canaan, **Baal** ➡

In Assyria, **Asshur**[1]

⬅ In Egypt, **Horus**
or **Harpocrates**[2] ➡

We even know how
Tammuz became a
"pretty boy," like
Adonis and **Attis**:

Attis of Phrygia

Adonis (Greece & Syria)

BUT DO YOU KNOW WHO *ELSE* TAMMUZ BECAME?

[1] Asshur as the sun god was the template for other "winged disk" gods: Anshar, Ashir, Asura, Ahura Mazda and Shamash—even the winged globe of Egypt.

[2] For more information on the Greek name Harpocrates (*Har-pe-khrad,* "Horus the Child" in Egyptian), see the End Note for page 67 in Appendix A.

TAKE A LOOK AT THESE FAMOUS GODS:

This little baby conquering the snakes in his crib is none other than **Hercules**. *Hmm*, a child bruising a serpent's head—where have we heard **that** before?[1]

The false god **Hercules** was very *adaptable*—almost as much as **Tammuz!** As a child and a young man, he *was* Tammuz. But look at his **strength**—it was like Nimrod's—or even Samson's! Do you know why?

YOU NEED TO KNOW AN IMPORTANT FACT:
Pagan gods didn't _just_ copy Babylon & Egypt. They *ALSO* copied actual Bible events and people!

So **Hercules copied Samson's life** in some of the later stories. Other gods followed as well. By the time the **Greeks** came to Egypt, they were **copying God's people** left and right!

Samson carrying the gates of Gaza and two posts. (Judges 16:3)

Hercules carrying two pillars at the strait of Gibraltar.

See Exodus 2:2; Acts 7:20 & Hebrews 11:23

For **baby Adonis** they **copied** the **true story** of beautiful **Moses** in a basket of bulrushes.

AND THE BLENDING OF GODS CONTINUED ...

[1] A similar story is told about Horus. See Gahlin, *Egyptian Religion* (2002), p. 61.

ANOTHER IMPORTANT FACT:
CHARACTERISTICS OF *ONE* "GOD" WERE OFTEN
CARRIED DOWN TO "SONS" AND "DAUGHTERS."

This means that after a while, you won't know
which you are talking about: **Cush, Nimrod** or **Tammuz!**

Hercules, for example, soon became a huge blend
of **Nimrod, Tammuz—*even Shem!* Check for yourself.**[1]

Just like most *goddesses* were known as **moon
goddesses**, so most *gods* were called **sun gods**, gods of
vegetation, heaven or the **underworld, creator**, even
mediator or **redeemer gods** at one time or other.

Out of just **five real
people** came **so many**
gods that <u>this</u> <u>book</u>
would have to be
bigger than the **New
York Phone Directory**
to tell about them!

—AND FINALLY WE COME TO THE MOST
IMPORTANT PART OF BABYLON RELIGION ...

---

[1] Just get a copy of Hislop's *Two Babylons* and read all the references to Hercules!

... AND IT ALL STARTED WITH A COW!

—Well, not *exactly*, but the cow **was** one of the **earliest** forms of Semiramis as a mother goddess. As **Ninsun** she became the **mother** of Gilgamesh![1] When she got to Egypt, she was *reworked* a little.

Note the **horns** (symbol of the crescent moon) and the **sun disc** inside.

NINSUN

Hathor

Believe it or not, this beauty is actually that **same** cow goddess! As **Hathor** (HATH-ore) she is the **mother of Horus**[2]—so she is really **Isis**. But in most Egyptian art, she has the **head** and **ears** of a cow as well. More and more, researchers are finding out that there are a **limited number of gods**— just a *whole lot* of **names**!

Aztec crescent moon (p. 88)

As you can see from this **Aztec crescent moon**, the horned symbol can be found all over the world.

Isis

From this "bovine beginning" came a whole "herd" of mother goddesses, each with a bratty child ...

---

[1] See pp. 28-31. See also Dalley, *Myths from Mesopotamia* (2000), pp. 51, 58-59, 61 & Turner & Coulter's *Dictionary of Ancient Deities* (2000), p. 348 under "Ninsun."

[2] In Egyptian, "hat-hor" means "house (or womb) of Horus." See Appendix A.

HERE ARE SOME MOTHER GODDESSES.
(See how many <u>you</u> recognize!)

These are **Isis & Horus:**	But so are **these:**	And so are **these:**

Coptic (Egyptian) drawing, 200s AD

Doesn't Horus seem a little **old** for nursing?

Here are others:

"Inanna & son" or "Ninhursag & Nesu"

Maya & Buddha

Devaki & Krishna

Indrani & child

Juno (Hera) & Hercules

Shing-Mu & son

BUT SATAN <u>STILL</u> HAD HIS BIGGEST PROBLEM ...

ONE DARK DAY IN SATAN'S LAIR:

Satan's **Babylon religion** was going **well**—perhaps *too well*. Once mankind got the idea, the gods multiplied like **rabbits**, and **new ones** were being made **every day**. This caused a *big problem* for his "**Semiramis scheme**." Follow along with the story and see for yourself!

MIDNIGHT:

NOW TO THE <u>HEART</u> OF THE MATTER!

Satan was *no dummy*—and he took <u>no</u> <u>chances</u>, either!
BUT THIS WASN'T HIS FINAL GOAL ...

---

[1] See also 1 Peter 1:9-12. God revealed about the sufferings of Christ to his prophets. Even angels knew (see verse 12). *They just didn't know the timetable!*

Satan drew his followers close, then said:

"You know how **my devils** are the **power** behind all the world's **statues, idols** and **images of gods.**[1] So *tell me...*"

---

[1] See Deuteronomy 32:16-17; Psalm 106:36-38; 1 Corinthians 10:19-21 & Revelation 9:20. Don't have a Bible handy? Read them in full in Appendix A!

"MY <u>WAFER</u> WILL BECOME THEIR <u>GOD</u>!!"

And this is **exactly** what priests did in ancient Egypt!

Pagans worshipped **lots** of gods made out of bread,

... but the WAFER GOD OSIRIS was most important...

[1] For amazing documentation of Egyptian and other wafer gods, see Appendix A!

... Because THIS god was shaped like the SUN![1]

It worked like a **charm** in Egypt! People believed **bread** had actually been turned into their **god**! Priests tried a **number** of shapes. **But *Satan's favorite*** was the **sun-shaped wafer of Osiris.** Its **power** was **incredible...**

IT WOULD HELP SATAN CONTROL THE EARTH!

Note the sun disk

Tammuz as sun god. Also known as Asshur, Ashir, Ahura Mazda & Shamash

Satan's plan: To make Tammuz (as the sun god) the *only* god worshipped by the <u>whole</u> <u>world</u>.

The plan was perfect—except for *one tiny little thing:*

What do we do with all the *other* gods and goddesses we created?

Hmm...

OOPS! NOW *THAT* WAS A PROBLEM!

[1] See Hislop, *The Two Babylons* (1858), p. 160.

As you have seen, behind every **idol** is a **devil**.[1] The devils are **spiritual** beings. They are **fallen angels**.[2] And just like the worst of us, they are **mean, cruel**—and most of all, **selfish!** There is *no way* they would **give up** their **power** over cities, communities, even **nations**. So the devils *behind* the idols fought each other to see who was the *most powerful "god" in the land*.

[1] See the footnote on p. 96.
[2] See Matthew 25:41; Revelation 12:7 & 9.

Note: The following may seem funny to you—but the Devil is *deadly serious* about taking your eyes off of God!

It was time for Satan to put his plan into action!

[1] For a historical example of this, see Hislop, *The Two Babylons* (1858), pp. 158-59.

With lots of people **moving** all over the earth and **competition** among cults, Satan's Babylon Religion began to spread far and wide.

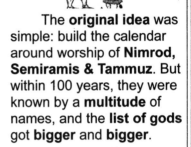

The **original idea** was simple: build the calendar around worship of **Nimrod, Semiramis & Tammuz.** But within 100 years, they were known by a **multitude** of names, and the **list of gods** got **bigger** and **bigger**.

Satan had a problem: how would he complete his **plan** to **replace God the Father** with **Semiramis**, **God the Son** with **Tammuz**, and **the Son of God's sacrifice** with the **sacrifice of Tammuz**? He needed to bring the people **back** to a **single concept**.

But *how* would he get pagans to worship just **one god (or goddess)** above all the others?

The solution was **simple**: make the **mother-goddess** the **center** of all religion. After all, who wouldn't want to have a "**kindly mother**" waiting to help them and answer their prayers? Satan was sure that his **trap was set**. But he *didn't* know **God was *about to act!***

ALL GOD NEEDED WAS <u>ONE</u> MAN <u>OF</u> FAITH ...

Chapter 4:

God's Plan for His People

Babylon was the **heart** of the ancient world. Its **doctrines** spread **far** and **wide**. There was **nowhere** that was left **untouched** by **Nimrod**, **Semiramis** and **Tammuz**. This was the literal **beginning** of "organized religion."

But Babylon Religion was *anything* but organized!

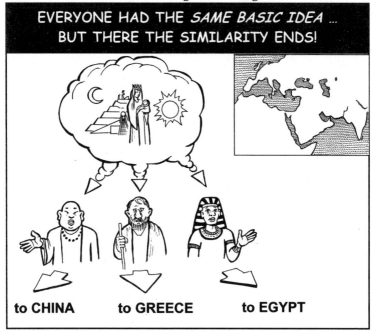

EVERYONE HAD THE *SAME BASIC IDEA* ...
BUT THERE THE SIMILARITY ENDS!

to CHINA   to GREECE   to EGYPT

As you remember, **God divided the languages** and those people **grouped into cities and cultures**. At first they **agreed**, since they all **knew** Nimrod, Semiramis and Tammuz **face to face**. But **unlike God's people**, who were careful to **write down God's words**, pagans passed stories down **orally** for the next generations. Then their legends and myths became a **secret** for paying customers to their cults. It wasn't until much **later** that they **wrote down** those **secret myths** and **ceremonies**.

BY THAT TIME THE *TRUTH* HAD BEEN TURNED INTO NOTHING BUT CONFLICTING *STORIES*!

And everyone said *his* story was the "original" one ...

Remember—the **"gods"** were all **devils in disguise!** And once they got their foothold in an area, they did **not** want to **leave** *or* **lessen their hold** on the people. So many cults and religions fought like cats and dogs, each claiming *his* god or goddess ruled the universe.

As a result, the myths and stories got even *more* mixed up. And to make matters worse, **new gods** (devils) were added, demanding **new** and **different ceremonies** and **sacrifices** to hold off *their* brand of evil or bring *their* kind of blessing. **WHAT A HORRIBLE MESS!**

Was the Devil *UPSET* about this? - Are you <u>kidding?</u>

SATAN _LOVED_ IT!!
Satan loves _anything_ that will get your mind off God!

Darkness spread upon the earth. Just like in the days before the Flood, the thoughts of man were **"only evil continually."**[1] And for close to **200 years** it looked like Satan had **won!** In time he would have his **one world religion** united in **worship** of **Semiramis** and her **child.**

— OR WOULD HE ? —

[1] See page 9 and Genesis 6:5.

WHEN HOPE WAS GONE, GOD CALLED A MAN: ABRAM (and *his* son Isaac and *his* son Jacob).

Abraham　　**Isaac**　　**Jacob**

Jacob begat **12 stubborn kids:**

Reuben　　Levi　　　Dan　　　Gad　　Issachar　　Joseph

　Simeon　　Judah　　Naphtali　　Asher　　Zebulon　　Benjamin

| From these came the nation of Israel, "God's chosen people" — | 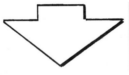 | These stiff-necked, hard-hearted and rebellious people were a mess, but: |

THEY WERE **BLESSED** BECAUSE OF **ABRAHAM!** WHY? SIMPLY BECAUSE HE *BELIEVED GOD*.[1]

God founded an *entire nation* because of the **faith** of **one man**. And soon the **Devil himself** would find out:

YOU DON'T MESS WITH GOD'S PEOPLE!

[1] See Genesis 15:4-6; Romans 4:3-5 and Galatians 3:6-9.

SATAN TRIED <u>MANY</u> <u>TIMES</u> TO ATTACK ISRAEL ...

... But as long as there were **praying men and women** who **loved God** and **believed His words** there was *nothing* the Devil could do to harm them.

Though at times they were totally *outnumbered*, Israel <u>defeated</u> their foes.

God *always* came to the aid of His faithful followers. *BUT*:

When they <u>rejected</u> God—Satan carried them captive.

God held off His judgment a *long time* ... But if they *still* didn't repent, He allowed Satan to take His people prisoner. And their new **masters** were **brutal**—so great was their **hatred** for God's people.

But God *still* held out His loving hand to them!

WHEN THEY REPENTED ... THEY WERE <u>RETURNED</u>!

God said it this way:
"… for I the LORD thy God *am* a jealous God, **visiting the iniquity of the fathers** upon the children unto the third and fourth *generation* **of them that hate me**, and **shewing mercy** *unto thousands of them that love me* and keep my commandments."[1]

Return to your homes.

We're sorry!

Forgive us, Lord!

Thank You, Lord!

This pattern continued for centuries, until Israel's Northern Kingdom fell to Assyria in 722 BC and those fateful years from 605-586 BC ...

After **years** of warnings by prophets of God, the southern kingdom of **Judah** finally fell to **Babylon** and the people were taken away captive.

Even Solomon's beautiful **Temple** was destroyed. **Many** in Israel **lost all hope**.

BUT GOD WASN'T FINISHED WITH THEM YET!

[1] See Deuteronomy 5:9-10.

AFTER 70 YEARS OF CAPTIVITY, GOD FULFILLED A WHOLE SET OF PROPHECIES AT ONCE!

I **had** them in my hands. What are you doing?

Return to **your** homes.

Rebuild your Temple.

Over 100 years before he was born, God called **Cyrus the** Persian to **capture** Babylon, **rescue** God's people and **command** the **rebuilding** of the **Temple** in **Jerusalem!** [1] Then in **445 BC** they began to **repair** the **wall** and the **city.** [2]

WHEN THEY REPENTED ... THEY WERE <u>RETURNED!</u>

In **516 BC** the Temple was **repaired**, though **nothing** like what it **had been** in **Solomon's** day. [3] The Devil was **furious!** He **couldn't stop it** from being **built**. And now **Messiah** was **coming.**

@!!!☆☆!

That should have been **MY** temple!

... And Satan's day was about to get a *lot* <u>worse</u>!

[1] God's prophecy about Cyrus is found in Isaiah 44:24-45:7. The prophecy of 70 years is found in Jeremiah 25:11; 29:1-14. Daniel prayed to God about it in Daniel 9.
[2] See Ezra and Nehemiah. Daniel 9:25 began God's prophetic clock, telling everyone (including the Devil) when "the Messiah the Prince" was to come. See Appendix A.
[3] See Ezra 3:10-13 and Haggai 2:1-3.

WHEN GOD'S PEOPLE LEFT, BABYLON FELL APART!

God punished **Babylon** for her sins against God's people.[1] The city of **Nimrod, Semiramis & Tammuz** was **left** to be slowly covered by the sands of history. By **122 BC** "the Great City" was mostly _ashes_!

BYE BYE, BABYLON!

No problem...

I'll just **move** my **Babylon Religion** somewhere **else**!

SATAN NEEDED A NEW CITY—AND FAST!

<u>Only</u> <u>one</u> <u>city</u> had shown the *potential* to become as **powerful** and **evil** as Babylon: Ancient Rome!

The Romans are vile, **vengeful**, greedy and **selfish**!

HEY! These guys are *MY* kind of people!

Rome was about to become Satan's NEW BABYLON!

[1] See Jeremiah 25:12; 50:18 and chapter 51. For a quick overview of what happened to Babylon after the days of Cyrus the Great, see Appendix A.

ONE MAN IN PARTICULAR CAUGHT SATAN'S EYE...

49-44 BC

No one's listening, **Julius**. *Say it again!*

I ... AM A GOD!

Hail Caesar! *HAW! HAW!*

Julius Caesar was a master **soldier** and **politician**. He was **so powerful** he <u>scared</u> the Roman senate! He ruled as a **tyrant** ... but after his *murder*, they **declared he was a god!** And soon after that, <u>all</u> emperors were said to be **gods**.

Satan was <u>thrilled!</u>

BUT HE KEPT A <u>WATCHFUL</u> <u>EYE</u> ON JERUSALEM.

In **21 BC** Satan was amazed to find King Herod began to **replace** the little Temple with a huge one *15 stories high!* Then he knew: **the <u>true</u> seed (child),** who would "bruise his head"—**God the son Himself**—was coming to earth ...

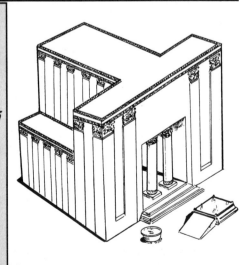

... AND WOULD SOON WALK IN HEROD'S TEMPLE!

Babylon was Satan's **throne**. From there he ruled the world. His religion of **Nimrod**, **Semiramis** & **Tammuz** spread across the globe. But his "organized religion" wasn't at all what it **appeared** to be.

His devils, masquerading as "gods" (idols), fought to be called the "**top god.**" So **not only cults** competed; **cities** and later even **countries** picked their "favorite" god or goddess to lead them all.

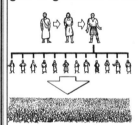

Into this confusion God called **Abram** who **believed Him**. He let his family become His own people: **Israel**, God's "**chosen nation.**" He **protected** them as long as they **trusted** Him. When they **rebelled**, His hand of protection **lifted**.

Even after Israel's **sins** piled up so high God had to kick them out of the land, it was **only** for a time. After **70 years**, God brought them back from **Babylon** itself! Then God set in motion the destruction of the ancient city of Babylon, **never** to be

Satan was **devastated**; he had to move quickly to create **another Babylon**: the ambitious city of **Rome**. He knew in a **few short years** the **true seed**—God the Son—would come to earth. **He _had_ to be ready…**

FOR THE <u>TRUE</u> FULFILLMENT OF THE PROPHECY!

Chapter 5:
The True Fulfillment of the Prophecy

One evening in **Galilee** about **5 BC**, an amazing event took place. **God** sent the **angel Gabriel** to a young Jewish virgin named Mary. He told her she would bear "the son of the Highest"—the Son of God Himself![1]

The **Holy Ghost** came upon her that night and put **God the Son** into her womb. **The Creator Himself, who made the universe,** was in the world like any human.[2] It **didn't** take long for the **forces of evil** to notice, either!

SATAN WAS ON HIGH ALERT. THE PROMISE OF GENESIS 3:15 WAS <u>FINALLY</u> BEING FULFILLED...

[1] See Luke 1:26-38.
[2] See John 1:10, 14.

THE EVIL POWERS IN ISRAEL WERE WORRIED ...

So **Satan waited it out.** Meanwhile **Jesus was born** in a time of year when shepherds **stayed out** at night with their flocks—**definitely NOT December 25th!!** [1] **Months later** wise men came to **Mary, Joseph** & **Jesus**...

BUT THE WISE MEN <u>ONLY</u> WORSHIPPED JESUS! [2]

[1] See Luke 2:8-20.
[2] See Matthew 2:1-12.

WHEN THE WISE MEN LEFT, SATAN MOVED ...

But God had already sent Jesus' family into Egypt![2]

An **angel of God** told Joseph to take his family and leave. **God preserved His Son**. Satan was **furious!**

Later on, when **Herod** was **dead**, the angel told them to go **back** to **Israel**. They settled in Nazareth.[3]

SATAN'S <u>FIRST</u> ATTACK FAILED MISERABLY!

[1] See Matthew 2:16-18.
[2] See Matthew 2:13-15.
[3] See Matthew 2:19-23.

JESUS' FAMILY WAS JUST LIKE ANY OTHER ...

... **Except** that **Jesus** was **God the Son!** He grew up with **four half-brothers**: James, Joses, Simon & Judas (Jude) and at least **two half-sisters.**[1] Mary was *blessed* by God—**not** left a **virgin!**[2] **Joseph** passed down his **carpenter's** skills, as was **custom** in Israel.

Joses

James

How do we know about Jesus' childhood? Because of these **two very clear scriptures:**

1 "...and **he** (Jesus) went down with them (Mary & Joseph), and **came to Nazareth**, and **was subject unto them**." (Luke 2:51)

Jude

Simon

2 "And **Jesus increased** in wisdom and stature, and **in favour with God and man**." (Luke 2:52)

Growing up like **any other Jewish boy** was the <u>only</u> way to gain such favor.

The Lord Jesus

WHEN JESUS GREW UP, EVERYTHING CHANGED!

[1] See Matthew 13:55-56; Mark 6:3. *Half*-siblings because **God** was *Jesus' Father!*
[2] Being barren was considered a *curse*, not a blessing. See Genesis 11:30; 25:21; 29:31; Exodus 23:26; Deuteronomy 7:14; Judges 13:2-3; Psalm 113:9 & Luke 1:7-25.

AT 30 YEARS OLD, JESUS BEGAN HIS MINISTRY...

Behold the **Lamb of God...**

Which taketh away the **sin** of the **world!**[1]

God had already shown John the Baptist the **Son of God's true mission**: to be the one **sacrificial lamb** to pay for the sin of mankind!

Remember: The **only** way a **lamb** takes away sin is by being **sacrificed** in a sinner's place.

Satan had to **stop** Jesus' ministry before it began. He knew of **three ways,** They *never* failed: "the lust of the **flesh**, the lust of the **eyes**, and the **pride** of life."[2]

Master, **Jesus might**—uh—be a *special case!*

NONSENSE! Jesus will be *no different* from the rest!

Ever since the **Garden of Eden,**[3] no man, woman, boy or girl could **resist** the **Devil's charms**.

But Satan was about to be *completely* disappointed!

[1] See John 1:29-33.
[2] See 1 John 2:16.
[3] See Genesis 3:1-6.

For 40 days the Devil tried to tempt Jesus[1], until ...

SATAN *FAILED*. HE WAS <u>FURIOUS</u>!!

Then he <u>left</u> Jesus—but ONLY for a while![3]

[1] See Matthew 4:1-9; Mark 1:13; Luke 4:2.   [3] See Luke 4:13.
[2] See Matthew 4:10.

DO YOU *REALIZE* WHAT JESUS <u>JUST</u> <u>SAID</u>?

The Lord Jesus, in what we call the **Sermon on the Mount** at the **beginning** of His ministry,[2] openly declared HE is the **JUDGE** on **DOOMSDAY**! He declared it in **simple language** for all "that have ears to hear":

THE LORD JESUS CHRIST <u>IS</u> <u>GOD</u> <u>ALMIGHTY</u>!

The Devil and his angels **knew** this was getting **out of control**. Satan had to act fast, or over **2,000 years of work** would go right down the drain. He decided:

It was time to tempt Him ... through His family!

[1] See Matthew 7:21-23.
[2] Found in Matthew 5-7.

SATAN HAD WATCHED JESUS' FAMILY CLOSELY.

Jesus' birth **less than 9 months** after Joseph wed Mary had been the talk of the town.[1] A **dark cloud** remained over Jesus all His life. Even **3 years** into His ministry, the scriptures quietly tell us the sad truth:

For neither did *his brethren* believe in him. (John 7:5)

Satan decided to **use this** against the Son of God. **One day as Jesus taught, someone came to the door...**

Mary & her kids had *no special access to Jesus!* What **matters** is being His **follower**—not His **family!**

JESUS <u>WASN'T</u> INTIMIDATED BY HIS RELATIVES. SATAN FAILED *AGAIN!*

[1] If your "inquiring mind" wants to *hear* this ancient gossip, see Appendix A!
[2] See Matthew 12:46-50.

This pressure would have <u>broken</u> any *ordinary* man.

... But **Jesus** was **no ordinary man.** He was **God Himself** in the **flesh!** No amount of **pressure** or **rejection** by the public—or even His own **brothers** and **sisters**—could get Him to **"lighten up"** or **change His mission** and **message.**

THE DEVIL TRIED <u>ONE</u> <u>MORE</u> <u>TIME</u>:

One day a woman lifted up her voice to Jesus and said:

Blessed is the *womb* that **bare thee, and the** *paps* which thou hast **sucked!**

That's my girl!

Yea <u>rather</u>, blessed are they that *hear the <u>word</u> of <u>God</u>,* and *<u>keep</u> <u>it</u>.* [1]

She wanted **Jesus** to exalt **Mary!**
This was **the** *essence* of Babylon Religion. [2]

BUT JESUS WASN'T FOOLED FOR A <u>SECOND</u>!

The Devil failed in **every attempt** to get Jesus to serve him. And Jesus **never** exalted Mary *or* His family.

**SATAN HAD <u>NO</u> <u>CHOICE</u> LEFT.
HE WAS <u>THROUGH</u> PLAYING GAMES ...**

[1] See Luke 11:27-28.
[2] See Hislop, *The Two Babylons* (1858), pp. 158-159 and pp. 101-104 of this book.

IT WAS TIME FOR JESUS TO <u>DIE</u>!

But Jesus was not afraid of them, because He "knew what was in man."[2] **He spoke boldly to the end ...**

... AND NOW THE END HAD FINALLY COME!

[1] See Deuteronomy 21:23.   [2] See John 2:25.   [3] See Matthew 23:33.

ON <u>ANY</u> <u>OTHER</u> PASSOVER IT LOOKED LIKE THIS:

All Jews, including the **high priest**, would choose a **spotless lamb** from among all the sheep to **sacrifice it** in their place for their sin. **Each family** chose one. The **high priest also** brought a lamb, parading it up to the Temple before the crowds **five days** before Passover.[1]

On **many occasions** in the Jewish year people cut down palm branches.[2] Here they waved them as they sang **Psalms 113-118** to remind them of **God's great deeds**—and of **Messiah** who would **save** them.[3]

BUT <u>THIS</u> PASSOVER WAS <u>NOT</u> LIKE <u>ANY</u> <u>OTHER</u>!

On **this same day** the long-awaited **Messiah**, the **eternal king of Israel** rode up to the city on a donkey, the symbol of a **king**.[4]

BUT THE PEOPLE OF JERUSALEM WERE IN FOR A <u>BIG</u> <u>SURPRISE</u>:

HE WAS <u>NOT</u> THE KIND OF KING THEY <u>EXPECTED</u>!

[1] See Exodus 12. This is called "Nisan (or Abib) 10" in the Jewish calendar.
[2] Especially the Feast of Tabernacles. See Leviticus 23:23-40 & Nehemiah 8:14-18.
[3] Known as the "Hallel" (Hebrew for "praise"). For more, see Appendix A.
[4] See John 12:1 & 12:12-19; Matthew 21:1-11; Mark 11:1-11 & Luke 19:28-40.

THE TRUE "LAMB OF GOD" HAD FINALLY ARRIVED!

(But all the **people** saw was an earthly **king**.)[1]

Blessed is the **king of Israel** ...

... that **cometh** in the **name** of **the Lord!**

Hosanna to the **son of David!**

Hosanna in the **highest!**

ON THIS DAY THE PROPHECY WAS FULFILLED:

"Rejoice greatly, O daughter of Zion;
shout, O daughter of Jerusalem:
behold, thy King cometh unto thee:
he *is* just, and having salvation;
lowly, and riding upon an ass,
and upon a colt the foal of an ass."
—Zechariah 9:9

In the **next day** Jesus **cleansed the Temple**.[2] Many thought that would **begin His reign**. But it *didn't!*

NO ONE UNDERSTOOD THE REAL REASON JESUS CAME TO JERUSALEM AT THE PASSOVER!

[1] See Matthew 21:9, 15; Mark 11:9-10; Luke 19:38 & John 12:13.
[2] See Matthew 21:12-13; Mark 11:11-18 & Luke 19:45-48.

THE PASSOVER LAMB WAS INSPECTED 4 DAYS. [1]

Believe me, I've checked this lamb over— **it is perfect and without blemish.**

Hmmm... Still—you **know** the **Law.**

Leave it tied outside so **everyone** can see **this lamb is pure!**

JESUS (THE LAMB) WAS ALSO INSPECTED 4 DAYS!

Which is the **first commandment of all?**

... in the **resurrection, whose wife** shall she be of the **seven?**

Master, we _**know**_ that thou art _**true**_...

By what authority doest thou these things?

...is it **lawful** to give **tribute** unto **Caesar**...

… or **not?**

JESUS ANSWERED EVERY QUESTION *PERFECTLY*. [2]
AFTER THIS *NO ONE* DARED ASK HIM ANYTHING!

[1] See Exodus 12:3-6 and the Babylonian Talmud, Volume 4, *Bavli Pesahim,* Folios 92B-99A, 9:1, Sections I.2C-D.

[2] See Matthew 21:16 - 22:46; Mark 11:18 - 12:34 & Luke 20:1-40. The scribes, chief priests, elders, Sadducees, Pharisees & Herodians all failed to find any sin in Him!

AT HIS LAST SUPPER, JESUS TOOK BREAD[1] ...

PLEASE NOTE: This **wasn't** Jesus' *actual flesh!*
1ˢᵗ Jesus was <u>right there</u> **with** <u>them</u>!
2ⁿᵈ Cannibalism was <u>against</u> <u>God's law</u>![2]

Jesus was **not** starting up a **new** pagan "bread-god" religion! **Communion** is to <u>remember</u> <u>what</u> **He** <u>did</u>. What was *about to happen to Him* was done **for our benefit.**

JESUS WAS ABOUT TO <u>GIVE</u> <u>HIS</u> <u>LIFE</u> ... FOR <u>US</u>!

[1] See 1 Corinthians 11:23-26; Matthew 26:26-29; Mark 14:22-25 & Luke 22:14-20.
[2] See Acts 10:14 & Leviticus 11. Human flesh is *not* in the list of "clean" foods!

In <u>hours</u> Jesus was tried, convicted and sentenced ...

... and was carrying the means of His own death!

Only days before, Jesus was their **Saviour and King**.
Now they yelled, CRUCIFY HIM!!

Only days before, people cried,
HOSANNA TO THE KING, THE SON OF DAVID!
Now they cried,
WE HAVE NO KING BUT CAESAR!

THIS WAS THE DARKEST DAY IN HISTORY:
WHEN GOD LET HIMSELF BE <u>MURDERED</u>
FOR CRIMES HE DID <u>NOT</u> COMMIT ...

FROM NOON TO 3 PM
JESUS HUNG ON THE CROSS.
IT WAS TIME FOR THE
PASSOVER SACRIFICE ...

[1] See Deuteronomy 21:23.
[2] See Gen. 3:15 & pp. 39, 95, 120 & 128 of this book.

At 3 PM, "at even,"[1] each family in Jerusalem took its own **chosen, pure, unspotted lamb** and **sacrificed it,** dipping a **hyssop branch** in the **blood of the lamb** ...

... then **struck** the **lintel** and **two doorposts** ...

... making the **prophetic shape** of a **cross!**[2]

At the same moment,
Jesus looked up to His Father in heaven and shouted ...

IT IS
FINISHED!

[1] The middle time between noon and nightfall. See Exodus 12:6-9 & Numbers 9:3.
[2] See Exodus 12:7 & 22.

IT IS FINISHED!

Suddenly the **thickly woven veil** of the Temple was torn, **from the top to the bottom,** as **unseen hands** laid open the way to the "holy of holies."

> GOD THE FATHER ACCEPTED HIS SON'S SACRIFICE TO PAY FOR SIN, <u>ONCE</u> <u>FOR</u> <u>ALL</u>! [1]

> AND THIS WAS ONLY THE BEGINNING! <u>NO</u> <u>ONE</u> WOULD FORGET THE *NEXT 3 DAYS* ...

[1] See Hebrews 9:12, 26-28; 10:10-14 & 1 Peter 3:18

In that <u>same</u> <u>moment</u>, an earthquake hit the city...

RUMBLE!

... and the graves began to open![1]

This would have caused **all sorts** of **problems**. They were beginning the 7 holy days called **"The Feast of Unleavened Bread,"** and **no unclean person** could **take part** in it. But to **re-bury the dead** would **make** you unclean![2] So the Jews had to **leave them sitting there.**

That's OK, because <u>God</u> <u>wasn't</u> <u>finished</u> with them!

[1] See Matthew 27:50-52a. The 2nd half of verse 52 happened *three days later.*
[2] See Numbers 19:11-22. They would be unclean exactly *seven days!*

THE NEXT MOMENT, JESUS SPOKE QUIETLY ...

Father, into thy hands I commend my spirit. [1]

Truly this man was the Son of God! [2]

"**Greater love** hath no man than this, that a man **lay down his life** for his friends." [3]

But Jesus laid down <u>His</u> life ... for His enemies!! [4]

When Jesus said **His last words**, He bowed His head ...

... AND HE DIED. THEN THEY BURIED HIM ...

[1] See Luke 23:46.
[2] See Matthew 27:54 & Mark 15:39.
[3] See John 15:13.
[4] See Romans 5:6-8.

THERE HIS BODY STAYED:

WEDNESDAY NIGHT,
THURSDAY,
THURSDAY NIGHT,
FRIDAY,
FRIDAY NIGHT,
SATURDAY, THEN —

BEFORE THE SUN ROSE SUNDAY MORNING ...

[1] See Matthew 12:38-40; 16:4 & Luke 11:29-30.
[2] See Matthew 27:62-66.

THE DEVIL WAS IN FOR A <u>RUDE</u> <u>AWAKENING</u>!

NOW where's His body?

He **tricked me!** I was **set up! WHO KNOWS** what He's up to now!!

GULP! I was **afraid** this would happen!

That night something **incredible** happened: **another** great earthquake hit Jerusalem as the angel of the Lord...

ROLLED AWAY THE STONE AND SAT ON IT!

The guards were so scared they **fainted!**[1] And after the risen Jesus left the tomb, they fled away in terror!

And they had good **reason**, too! For when **Jesus** rose from the tomb, so did a lot of **other people!**[2] Remember those **graves** that were opened (p. 138)? **It must've scared the people to death!**

AND <u>STILL</u> GOD WASN'T DONE!

[1] See Matthew 28:1-8; Mark 16:1-9a; Luke 24:1-9; John 20:1-18.
[2] Read *again* Matthew 27:51-53!

THE RISEN SAVIOUR'S TIME WAS SHORT, SO HE GAVE HIS FINAL INSTRUCTIONS—FOR *40 DAYS!* [1]

All **power** is given unto me in heaven and in earth. [2]

Go ye into all the world, and **preach the gospel** to every creature. [3]

I can see His **nail prints!**

He that **believeth** ... shall be **saved**; but he that **believeth not** shall be **damned.** [4]

Go ye therefore, and teach all nations ... [5]

And this wasn't all! Then Jesus opened His apostles' minds so they could **understand the whole Bible!** [6] The whole plan of God now made **perfect sense** to these chosen vessels.

OVER 500 PEOPLE AT ONCE SAW THE RISEN JESUS[7]... BUT THE BEST WAS YET TO COME!

[1] See Acts 1:1-3.
[2] See Matthew 28:18.
[3] See Mark 16:15.
[4] See Mark 16:16.
[5] See Matthew 28:19.
[6] See Luke 24:45.
[7] See 1 Corinthians 15:3-7.

AFTER THIS, JESUS ASCENDED TO HEAVEN ... *BEFORE THEIR VERY EYES!* [1]

This was **no magic trick!** In front of **many witnesses**, Jesus **visibly** went up until a cloud received Him out of their sight. Then as they gazed into heaven...

Two angels told them **Jesus** will come back **in the same way** He went into heaven! [2] When He returns, He'll bring His saints (followers) back **with Him!** [3]

Blast it! If I **knew** He'd rise from the dead, I **never** would have had Him **crucified!** [4]

Why didn't you **tell me** this would happen?

You let Him **escape** out of our **hands!**

This is all **YOUR fault, IDIOT!**

Sheesh! I just **can't win** with this guy!

THE WAY TO HEAVEN WAS FINALLY OPENED ...

[1] See Mark 16:19 & Luke 24:51.
[2] See Acts 1:2, 9-11.
[3] See Zech. 14:3-9; Jude 1:14 & Revelation 19:14.
[4] See 1 Corinthians 2:8.

I am <u>the</u> <u>way</u>, the truth and the life:

<u>no</u> <u>man</u> cometh unto the Father, <u>but</u> <u>by</u> <u>me</u>. [1]

Just like the **Temple's torn veil opened the way** to the **most holy place,** so **Jesus' broken body** opened the way to be reconciled with **God the Father in heaven.** [2]

Now **anyone** may come directly to God the Father, but **only** through **His Son, the Lord Jesus Christ.** There is <u>no</u> <u>other</u> <u>way</u>—not through **Mary, Joseph, Buddha** or **anyone else** [3]—*only* faith in the **shed blood of Jesus.**

[1] See John 14:6.
[2] See Hebrews 10:19-25.
[3] See Acts 4:12; 1 Timothy 2:5

EVERY PRIEST IS JUST ANOTHER HUMAN BEING:

Jewish priests shared certain characteristics:
- **They all sinned.**
- **They all died.**
- **They all were <u>only</u> priests <u>until</u> they died.**

But Jesus is unlike ANY priest known to mankind!
- **He never sinned.**
- **He became High Priest *after* He died! And rose!**
- **He <u>never</u> hands over His priesthood to <u>anyone</u>!**

Jesus is our **only** High Priest.[1] And **we who believe** in Him are **all priests to God!**[2] We may all **equally** go to God the Father—so **why** do we need any **more** priests?

ANSWER: WE <u>DON'T!</u>

BUT—HAVEN'T WE BEEN TOLD THAT THERE ARE <u>OTHER</u> LADDERS TO HEAVEN?

[1] See Hebrews 2:17-18; 4:14-16; 5:1-10; 6:20-7:28; 8:1-6; 9:1-28.
[2] See 1 Peter 2:5-10 & Revelation 1:6; 5:10.

Yes, there are **all <u>sorts</u> of saints and angels and apostles**, who will **gladly** "lead you to Jesus." And many have their **own "ladders to heaven"** to help you!

DON'T YOU BELIEVE IT!

I am the door of the sheep. [1]

He that entereth not by the door into the sheepfold, but climbeth up some other way, the same is a <u>thief</u> and a <u>robber</u>. [2]

Those aren't *really* saints and apostles and angels ...

THEY ARE ALL DEVILS IN DISGUISE!

Don't let them con you! Their purpose is to **trick you** into believing there are **many ways** to heaven! *It's a lie!*

In the End, **every one of us** must appear before the **throne** of **Jesus Christ**, either as our **Saviour** [3] ...

OR AS OUR JUDGE [4] ...

[1] See John 10:7.
[2] See John 10:1.
[3] See Romans 14:10 & 2 Corinthians 5:10.
[4] See Revelation 20:11-15.

AT JUDGMENT DAY MANY WILL SAY TO JESUS:

Lord! Lord!

Have we not **prophesied** in thy name?

And in thy name have **cast out devils?**

And in thy name **done many wonderful works?**

I *never* knew you! *Depart* from me, ye that work iniquity. [1]

DO YOU WANT TO HEAR THESE WORDS?

These "spiritual giants" were just **religious phonies!**
These big-shots will face a <u>holy</u> and <u>righteous</u> <u>God</u>
who will <u>judge</u> them according to their <u>works</u>. [2]

BUT YOU DON'T HAVE TO HEAR THIS ...

[1] See Matthew 7:21-23.
[2] See Revelation 20:11-15.

Satan was in *big trouble!* The Promised Seed of the woman, God the Son, was coming to earth. Satan hated Jesus and wanted to kill Him. But God was always **one step ahead of Satan** (at least!) So Satan went to Plan #2:

Satan tried to **tempt** Jesus. But that failed miserably, as well. What can you give the Man who has *everything*—literally? The Lord Jesus passed *every* test the Devil threw at Him and clearly **rejected** Babylon religion!

But the Devil *thought* he got the last laugh: he had Jesus betrayed, tried, beaten and crucified. He also wanted God the Father to curse His Son—and **stop** the prophecy of Gen. 3:15 from coming true. So Satan bruised **Jesus'** head—so it *seemed!*

Three days later, **the Lord Jesus Christ rose from the dead**, *ruining* Satan's plans! Then He spent **40 days preparing His disciples** to spread God's words throughout the world. Then He went **back** to heaven in the sight of **witnesses**, with the **promise** He'd **return** in the **End**.

Jesus is our "great High Priest," the "door of the sheep," "the Way, the Truth and the Life." There is *no other way* to heaven but through **Jesus Christ**. All our religious works are **nothing** to Him. We *must* be saved **by faith** in Him **alone!**

Satan was <u>defeated</u>. But the war had *only* <u>*started!*</u>

Chapter 6:

From Nero to Constantine

The gospel spread steadily till the Summer of 64 AD...

Then a **fierce fire** blazed through Rome, burning up **almost 3/4** of the city, over **6 days** and **7 nights**. Up till then **Christianity** was seen as a branch of **Judaism**. But **something changed** as **Nero** was said to be playing his lyre:

> Oh, I **love** to play music by a nice warm **fire!**

> **Look**—say those no-good **Christians** set it. You'll get off scot-free!

> **Good idea!**

Nero **quickly** blamed the **Christians** for setting the fire. The response was **immediate**. **Persecutions** began. Nero **lighted** Christians on fire, publicly **tortured** them, and had them **killed for sport** at the **Roman Circus,** on a little-known hill by the name of **Vaticanus!** [1]

> The more I **kill** them, the more they **multiply!** I've **got** to find a **better way** to **destroy** them!

The Caesars **slaughtered** the new believers, but **the words of God** kept **spreading** over the whole Roman empire! Satan was **stumped!** What could he <u>do</u> to **stop** the Christians?

Meanwhile in Antioch ...

[1] See Appendix A for more information.

Antioch was a *gathering place* for God's words.

The Bible says **Antioch of Syria** was the *first* place where the **disciples** were known as **"Christians."**[1] It was also a **gathering place** for the words of God. **Before 120 AD** the Bible books as we know them had been **collected** there and were **ready** to be **translated** into **every language** under heaven![2] Travelers from **all over the empire** passed through this important town.

SO GOD DECIDED TO TRANSLATE HIS HOLY, PRESERVED WORDS IN ANTIOCH!

Lord, it's amazing! He's translating it perfectly!

Of course ... I am helping him.

By 157 AD the Old Latin Bible (and other translations) had **already** begun to cover **Europe**. The Bible **didn't** need a **committee** to **decide** they were God's words—only men & women of **faith** to **translate** and **copy** them!

Jesus <u>kept</u> His promise!

"Heaven & earth shall pass away, but <u>my</u> <u>words</u> shall not pass away."[3]

IF YOU WERE THE DEVIL, WHAT WOULD <u>YOU</u> DO?

---

[1] See Acts 11:26.
[2] See Daniels, *Did the Catholic Church Give Us the Bible?* (2005), Chapter 2.
[3] See Matthew 24:35; Mark 13:31 & Luke 21:33.

What else? GO BACK TO EGYPT!

"Professing themselves to be wise, they became fools"
—Romans 1:22

The Devil once used the Egyptians to **re-invent** the Babylon story. That was a *huge success*. But now ...

SATAN WANTED TO DO SOMETHING <u>MUCH</u> <u>BIGGER</u> THAN HE'D *EVER* DONE ...

[1] See Daniels, *Did the Catholic Church Give Us the Bible?* (2005), pp. 32-39.
[2] See Appendix A for more information on *the missing verses of Mark (16:9-20)!*

312 AD, just outside Rome: Two men, Constantine and Maxentius, battle for control of the empire ...

SO THE DEVIL GAVE HIM WHAT HE ASKED FOR:

Constantine then told **everyone** his **vision!** (Well, that's what they **thought** he did, anyway.) You have to **remember:** This guy was a **religious politician.** *BEWARE!!*

WATCH HIM AS HE WEAVES HIS LIES ...

[1] Latin, *Sol Invictus*, also called Helios, Apollo, Shamash, etc. See Appendix A.

Nobody was more **vague** than Constantine! As he told *supposedly* the **same story** to different people, each person had his *own idea* of what the vision **meant!**

In a short time, all sorts of **different** "crosses" were designed, each saying it was "Constantine's cross:"

From a 300s AD coffin.

Believe it or not, these are modified PAGAN symbols! [1]

AND CONSTANTINE WAS <u>DEFINITELY</u> A PAGAN!

[1] See Appendix A for more information on these pre-Christian symbols!

CONSTANTINE WORSHIPPED THE <u>SUN GOD</u> —NOT <u>GOD</u> THE <u>SON</u>!

Two years earlier, in **310 AD**, he claimed he saw a vision of the **sun god Apollo** and publicly **made vows** to **serve him**. And as soon as Satan gave him **victory** over **Maxentius**, he went **back** to that shrine ...

...to thank <u>Apollo</u>—not Jesus Christ—for his victory![1]

APOLLO
(TAMMUZ)

From ancient writings we can see that Constantine worshipped the **sun god** in **many forms**: **Mithras** (a god of Persia popular with Roman soldiers) **Sol Invictus**, **Helios** and **Apollo**, among others.[2] Of course, *we all know* who all these sun gods *really* were: Semiramis' kid **Tammuz!**

But he was about to be worshipped under a <u>new</u> name!

[1] See Michael Grant, *Constantine the Great* (1993), pp. 131-32 and James Carroll, *Constantine's Sword* (2001), pp. 180-81.
[2] See the End Note for p. 155 in Appendix A for details.

SATAN WHISPERED INTO CONSTANTINE'S EAR ...

Connie baby, we **both** know you worship the **sun god**, but you've got to **pretend** to be a **Christian**!

Trust me ... It will pay off, **big time!**

I've got it! I'll put a stop to persecution of Christians …

I must be a genius!

Yeah, you're **brilliant.** Now here's how you will set up Catholicism as Rome's **new religion** …

A gradual change began to take place.

Instead of the "sun god," people began to worship a god called "Jesus Christ," which pleased Christians—

Jesus depicted as the sun god pulling his chariot across the sky. From 3rd century sarcophagus in Vaticanus hill.

This coin, minted by Constantine 313-321 AD reads "*SOLI INVICTO COMITI*" (To the Sun, my unconquerable companion).

—But it wasn't *really* Jesus Christ, was it?

GREAT CHANGES WERE UNDERWAY. CONSTANTINE HAD ONLY BEGUN TO FORM ROME'S *NEW* BABYLON RELIGION.

AS EARLY AS 313 AD, CONSTANTINE BELIEVED THE "CHURCHES" WERE UNDER <u>HIS</u> CONTROL ... [1]

... <u>*CATHOLIC*</u> CHURCHES, THAT IS!

Now Constantine set about **converting the masses.**
Hmm... I wonder why his "church" **grew so fast?**

AND HIS POWER KEPT GROWING.

[1] For this section see Grant, *Constantine the Great* (1993), pp. 156-86 and Carroll, *Constantine's Sword* (2001), pp. 184-93.

CONSTANTINE KEPT PASSING MORE LAWS ...

Constantine had become **ruler** of this early Catholic religion.

But to favor *Catholics, he* had to **suppress** all **true Christians & the Jewish people**, and force them to obey **man's** laws instead of **God's!** God's people saw the "writing on the wall" and left Rome.

Satan's new church showed its hatred for the Jews.

THEN SATAN ATTACKED BIBLE-BELIEVERS ...

... WITH HIS <u>COUNTERFEIT</u> <u>BIBLE</u>!

These Bibles didn't even **agree** with each other! But **Eusebius of Caesarea** took them to Rome, **anyway.**[1]

With his **counterfeit church** growing at a rapid pace, Satan didn't **need** Constantine anymore ...

IT WAS TIME TO SAY "GOODBYE" TO CONNIE!

[1] See Daniels, *Did the Catholic Church Give Us the Bible?* (2005), pp. 32-38 & 46.

As usual, Satan appealed to Constantine's huge pride:

You're **too big** for **Rome.** You need a **new city** … with *your own name on it!*

What a **great idea!** I'll start packing.

I'm going to call my new city **Constantinople** … after **myself!**

Then I'll take my **kids—Constantine, Constantius & Constans—with me** to Constantinople!

In short, **Constantine bought it,** *hook,* line *& thinker!*

330 AD:

EASTWARD HO! ONWARD TO **BYZANTIUM!**[1]

That gets him out of **Rome.** *Good riddance!*

ALL THE FOUNDATIONS WERE LAID. NOW BABYLON RELIGION WOULD BE FULLY RESTORED!!

[1] See Daniels, *Did the Catholic Church Give Us the Bible?* (2005), pp. 48-49.

Persecution and killing Christians couldn't stop the gospel from spreading. Satan was **powerless** to prevent the **whole world** from hearing about how the Lord Jesus Christ offers to save and forgive **everyone** who **believes** in Him.

And in Antioch of Syria God's words were being **faithfully preserved** in **accurate translations** and **perfect copies** of those translations. In **under 100 years** they covered the **empire!**

So Satan went back to **Egypt** and used his "scholars" to **rewrite the Bible**. They **took away** from God's words and created a monstrous *new* Bible. This would be the foundation for perverted Bibles of the future.

Now he needed a man to **link** Egypt with Rome and begin to **integrate** the sun god with Christianity. That man was **Constantine**. Constantine worshipped the sun god, but was a **religious politician**— the best combination Satan could ask for! Soon he **united** his empire in the worship of the sun god, whom he renamed **Jesus**.

Everyone fell for it—*except* the **Bible-believing** Christians and Jews! Christians fled Rome. Jews began to be persecuted as Christ killers and the Devil was happy. But there was *still* one more step to go before the transforming of Babylon Religion was complete ...

SEMIRAMIS HAD TO RUN THE *WHOLE SHOW*!

Chapter 7:

Babylon Religion—Revived!

ONE DAY THE DEVIL WAS PREOCCUPIED ...

Why are you reading the **Bible**, Master?

... It _**must**_ be in here **some**place!

Satan's Babylon Religion was **not yet** _**complete**_. It had to **look** just like a Bible-believing church, yet still **revive** the ancient religion of **Nimrod**.

More books, Chief.

I've got the **sun god** renamed "Jesus," a religion in Rome... what am I _**missing**_?

I know!

Pick _me!_

_I_ **know!** I'll make a **form** of **Semiramis**...

Semiramis!

...*everyone* can worship!

Human sacrifice!

You **did** it **again**, Chief!

What could Satan be up to?

NEXT: THE DEVIL'S KIND OF CHURCH!

For this, Satan needed something from <u>every</u> religion.

Then he dumped them all together into the Vatican ...

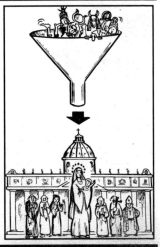

And PRESTO! A whole new "Christian-like" religion!

You're about to see how Satan fit it all together ...

(Drum roll, please) ... THE WAFER GOD!

Behold! Nothing up my sleeve ... **nothing** but **me** and this **sun-shaped wafer**. (And a little wine... I get *thirsty*, you see.)

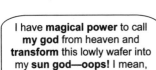

I have **magical power** to call **my god** from heaven and **transform** this lowly wafer into my **sun god—oops!** I mean, the Son of God. *Trust me!*

"**Jesus**," when I say the **magic words**, you **drop** on down out of heaven and **pop** into this **cookie**!

(**Trust** me. This works *every time!*)

GET READY FOR THE MAIN EVENT!

Hocus-pocus! Uh ... I mean, *Hoc Est Enim Corpus Meum* ..

(I'll bet you didn't know that "This is my body" becomes **magical** when said in **Latin** by a **priest!**)

Okay, **here I come**, ready or not!

Here, eat this. This is *no longer* bread. This is now the body, soul and divinity of your **god.**[1]

This "miracle" is known as *transubstantiation*. Look **familiar?**

I feel so **holy!** I just **ate God!** What an *experience!*

Next!

[1] Look familiar? If not, please reread p. 97! See also Jack T. Chick, *Smokescreens* (1983). *Read it online at www.chick.com!*

Note: We are not **blaspheming Catholicism. They** are blaspheming *Jesus!* Remember that **important fact** ...

BEHIND EVERY IDOL IS A <u>DEVIL</u>!! [1]

All around the world at **this very minute** men, women & children are being **fed** a **wafer god** that Roman Catholics call "Jesus." They **bow** to it, **pray** to it, **talk** to it and **eat it up**, believing they have "**received Christ.**"

BUT <u>NOTHING</u> COULD BE FURTHER FROM THE TRUTH!

They are partaking of _devils_ (1 Corinthians 10:21).

All these idols are an <u>abomination</u> to the Lord: [2]

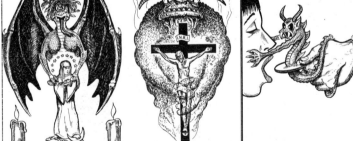

And more abominations are committed daily ...

[1] Read again Deuteronomy 32:16-17; Psalm 106:36-38; 1 Corinthians 10:19-21 & Revelation 9:20. They are also in the Appendix A note for p. 96.
[2] See Lev. 26:1; Deut. 7:25-26; 27:15; 1 Cor. 5:11; 6:9; 10:7, 14 & 1 Thess. 1:9.

Precious Roman Catholics are being deceived and bilked out of their money by leaders, who themselves are "deceiving, and being deceived" (2 Timothy 3:13).

The Lord Jesus said:

"...call **no man your father** upon the earth: for one is your Father, which is in heaven." —Matthew 23:9

How many **other** sins do you see in this picture?

AND *JUST IN CASE* ANYONE <u>DARED</u> TO FIND OUT THE TRUTH OF THE BIBLE ...

Origen's perverted Bible (with a few minor revisions)
was translated into Latin as
the "new Babylon's" (Rome's) Bible...
REJECTING THE PRESERVED WORDS OF GOD!

THE CATHOLIC NOOSE WAS BEGINNING
TO TIGHTEN AROUND THE WHOLE WORLD ...

For **all nations** have drunk of the wine of the wrath of her fornication, and the **kings of the earth** have committed fornication with her, and the **merchants of the earth** are waxed rich through the abundance of her delicacies. —Revelation 18:3

She is also known as "THE MOTHER OF HARLOTS" [1] (false religions) ...

INCLUDING A UNIQUE LITTLE RELIGION CALLED...

[1] See Revelation 17:5

And "Sin" became "Allah"...

THEN MUHAMMAD BECAME ALLAH'S "PROPHET" ...

This is the **final revelation** of **Allah!**

The **Qur'an**[1] is the compiled group of visions given to Muhammad by a **devil** calling himself "The angel **Gabriel**."[2]

Satan set up a **new religion**, dedicated to fighting, killing and **male-dominating** the world.

The *Qur'an* (and their multi-volume book of sayings of Muhammad, the *Hadith*, even say **Jesus** served Allah (that pagan moon god)!

How could a *goddess* sneak her way into <u>this</u> religion?

Lo! **Allah** is **my Lord** ....

Lo! **I am** the **slave of Allah.**

Muslim "Jesus" | Qur'an 3:46-59 & 19:30-32.

ANSWER: Easy!! As the "Virgin Mary" !!

Believe it or not, the *Qur'an* & *Hadith* say Mary was an *unmarried virgin,*[3] free from *all sin,*[4] who "reached the level of perfection" !![5]

"MARY" IS THE <u>KEY</u>!!

---

[1] For more on the *Qur'an*, see Morey, *Islamic Invasion*, chapters 8-10 & the Caners' *Unveiling Islam,* chapter 4..

[2] A *devil*, not an angel, guided Muhammad. Read Galatians 1:6-9!

[3] See the Caners' *Unveiling Islam*, pp. 203, 213 & 215.

[4] See the *Qur'an*, Surah 3:42; 5:75 & Tetlow, et. al., *Queen of All*, p. 33.

[5] See the *Hadith* of Sahih Bukhari, Volume 4, Book 55, #642-643.

BUT SATAN HAD <u>ANOTHER</u> TRICK UP HIS SLEEVE:

Note the **crescent moon & Venus.**

Muhammad & Fatima

Muhammad had a favorite daughter: **FATIMA**. He said she was the "highest woman in paradise" —*after Mary, of course!*[1]

So when Semiramis (as "The Virgin Mary") showed up in Portugal, what **city** do you think Satan chose for the "miracle?"

You guessed it! <u>FATIMA</u>!!

Semiramis had them in the **palm** of her **hand!** They started to visit "Virgin Mary" shrines *around the world!*[2]

NOW TAKE A <u>BIG</u> GUESS:

How will **Satan** <u>unite</u> Islam with **Roman Catholicism?**

[1] See Martin Lings, *Muhammad: His Life Based on the Earliest Sources* (1983), p. 329; Tetlow, *et. al.*, *Queen of All* (2006), p. 36; Crusaders Vol. 17, *The Prophet* (1988), p. 27; *Don Sharkey, The Woman Shall Conquer* (1976), p. 164. Also see the *Hadith* of Sahih Bukhari, Vol. 4, Book 56, #819. (See the quote in Appendix A.)
[2] See Francis Johnston, *Fatima: The Great Sign* (1980), Chapter 13 &Tetlow, *et.al, Queen of All*, Chapter 3.

WITH "VISIONS OF MARY" — *WHAT ELSE?*

The **Qur'an** says **Mary & her son** are for a "sign,"[1]—*and* that **Allah** will give **signs** that *Muslims will recognize* before the end of the world.[2]

On October 13, **1917,** 70,000 people watched the **sun** over **Fatima** seem to **fall** from the sky and return.

The three shepherd children of Fatima, "Mary" & the "Dancing Sun"

MANY BECAME CATHOLICS!

Satan knows "the **Virgin Mary**" is the **key** to bring **Muslims** into **Babylon Religion:**

Before the **Second Coming of Christ, Mary must**, more than ever, **shine** … in order **to bring unbelievers** into the **Catholic Faith.** …. Mary will extend the reign of Christ **over the heathens and Mohammedans** ….[3]

"Saint" Mary of Agreda, 17th century Catholic mystic

Missionaries … among the **Muslims** will be **successful** in the measure that they **preach Our Lady of Fatima**.

… [Islam] … will eventually be converted to Christianity …through a summoning of the **Muslims** to a **veneration** of the **Mother of God**.[4]

Archbishop Fulton J. Sheen (1895-1979)

And there are a lot of "Marys" to spread around …

[1] See the *Qur'an*, Surahs 21:91-93 & 23:50-54.
[2] Also called "portents." See the *Qur'an*, Surahs 27:93; 41:53 & 54:1-2.
[3] See Appendix A for full quotations. See also Tetlow, *et. al., Queen of All*, pp. 35-36.
[4] See Fulton Sheen, *The World's First Love: Mary, Mother of God* (1952), Chapter 17.

ALL OVER THE WORLD YOU FIND "VIRGIN MARY" GODDESSES TO FIT <u>EVERY</u> CULTURE & LANGUAGE:

The earth is filled with a multitude of Marys: Asian, African, Latin American ... something for *everybody!*

... AS LONG AS YOU BELONG TO THE <u>POPE</u>!!

SATAN'S SYSTEM WAS NOW FULLY SET UP!

Look at what I've given you:
- A *goddess* and her *kid*
- A *god* you can *eat*
- A **new** *Bible*
- The **most** *powerful* religious force in *history!*

Don't insult me by *refusing* all I've done!

Because if you **do,** we have **ways** to make you *pay.*

To keep people in line, Satan invented a useful little procedure known as: THE INQUISITION!

Ugh! What **stinks?** It smells **awful!**

What smell?

It's just the **tiny little Inquisition.**

We don't **talk** about it.

Big deal! It was only a **blip** on the **screen** of **history!**

Only 3,000 died…

Leave it alone!

TOP SECRET
DO NOT OPEN !

NO WAY!

It's time to *blow open the lid* and <u>reveal</u> the <u>secret</u>!

SATAN'S KILLERS BEGAN THEIR BLOODY WORK.

The **Inquisition** began in the early 1200s—as a very **secretive** operation. No news media **exposed** this **religious terrorism**. Only **quiet whispers** penetrated the silence of these **secret police**. They came for you at _**any time**_, day or night.

No one dared _oppose_ this **killing machine!**

The popes said this was "of God" ... but _which god?_

Napoleon Bonaparte
(1769-1821)

Between **1220** and **1809 AD** **unspeakable crimes** were committed against those who **refused** to bow & **worship Semiramis & Tammuz**— cleverly **disguised** as **Mary & Jesus!**

God used **Napoleon** to **order** the **Inquisition** to **stop** its tortures. _But the order was not carried out..._

..._until_ a **colonel** was <u>attacked</u> by two **Inquisition guards!** **2 regiments** assembled outside their **Catholic fortress.**

IT WAS <u>WAR</u> AGAINST THE INQUISITION! [1]

---

[1] The following account comes from Jean Paul Perrin, *History of the Old Albigenses* (around 1618), Book 2 Appendix, found in Ages Software's *Master Christian Library*.

5 miles out of Madrid, Napoleon's forces approached ...

Open the gates of the Inquisition ... Surrender to the imperial army!

BANG!!

I'm hit!

Suddenly the sentinel **shot** one of the **soldiers!** The army was forced to **attack.** Soon **well-hidden forces fired** upon them, as the soldiers used a **ram** to **force** their way into the citadel.

UNBELIEVABLE!
The **Inquisitor General** and his **"father confessors"** pretended **nothing** had happened!

Friends, this is **all a** misunderstanding!

Stop! Do not desecrate our holy house!

They searched in vain for **any** implements of torture. But the colonel was *not done.* He ordered **water** to be poured on the **floor**—and where it **seeped down** he discovered **a hidden __door__** going beneath the fortress!

YOU WON'T __BELIEVE__ WHAT THEY *DISCOVERED!*

... AND WE'RE NOT GONNA SHOW YOU, EITHER!

What the soldiers found is _**too horrible**_ to print in this book. Only **devilish minds** could conjure such **unimaginable tortures!** But for the **Roman Catholic system** to call itself a **"Christian organization"** ...

IT'S _OUTRAGEOUS!_

The **Inquisition** played **no favorites. Children** were torn from their mothers' arms, & **women** with **unborn children** suffered **unspeakable pains.**

... and no one listened to their screams for mercy!

Jesus said, "**Love** your **enemies, bless** them that **curse** you, **do good** to them that **hate you,** and **pray for** them which **despitefully use** you, and **persecute** you." [1]

DOES <u>THIS</u> LOOK LIKE _LOVE?_

[1] See Matthew 5:44.

What Napoleon's men did next **broke the back of the Inquisition!** They **released** those **tortured souls**—from 14 to 70 years old, all naked and chained—**clothed** them and carefully **brought** them into the light of day. Soon thousands heard the "Inquisition" was **no more!**

The **next** sounds to be heard were the **explosion** of the citadel and the **thundering** "Hallelujahs" as it **blew to bits** before the people's eyes.

BETWEEN 1220 AND 1809,
OVER 50 MILLION WERE MARTYRED FOR CHRIST. [1]

Is the Inquisition over and done with?
DON'T YOU BELIEVE IT!
It is **in hiding**, waiting for the **Beast** of **Revelation** to rear his **ugly head**.

TODAY ALMOST ALL RELIGIOUS, POLITICAL,
ECONOMIC [2] **& EVEN EVANGELICAL**
ORGANIZATIONS
SEEK THE BLESSING OF ROME.

SO WHO'S _REALLY_ IN POWER?

[1] See David Plaisted, "Estimates of the Number Killed by the Papacy in the Middle Ages" available online.
[2] For an eye-opener, see F. Tupper Saussy, *Rulers of Evil* (1999), pp. 1-4.

With whom **the kings of the earth have committed fornication**, and the inhabitants of the earth have been **made drunk** with the **wine** of **her fornication**. —Revelation 17:2

Semiramis, I could *never* have done all this without you!

I'll drink to that! (HIC!)

"And I saw the woman <u>drunken</u> with the *blood of the saints*, and with the *blood of the martyrs of Jesus*" —Revelation 17:6

"And *in her* was found the <u>blood</u> of the *prophets*, and of the *saints*, and of <u>*all*</u> *that were slain upon the earth*." —Revelation 18:24

... AND <u>THAT</u> WAS WHY SATAN CREATED HER!

The lord Jesus **hates** this **evil system**,
"that great city, which reigneth over the kings of the earth."
And He will **destroy her before His Second Coming**. [1]

> **"Babylon the great is fallen, is fallen,
> and is become the habitation of devils,
> and the hold of every foul spirit,
> and a cage of every unclean and hateful bird."
> —Revelation 18:2**

One day all heaven will shout,
"**...**true and righteous *are* his judgments: for he hath
judged the **great whore**, which did **corrupt the earth** with
her fornication, and hath **avenged the blood** of his
servants at her hand."—Revelation 19:2

AND BABYLON RELIGION WILL BE <u>NO</u> <u>MORE</u>!!

[1] See Revelation 17:16 through chapter 18.

The **powers of darkness rule** behind this papal throne.
They have led **billions** of **precious souls**
into the Lake of Fire.

All this **beauty** and **gorgeous ceremony** may give
you "**religious goosebumps,**" but it will cost you eternity.
You must **flee** from this **religious monster**, and **run into
the arms** of God the Son and **Son of God**, the Lord
Jesus Christ. _Heaven_ or _hell_, the choice is _yours_.

"**Come unto me**, all ye that **labour** and are **heavy laden**,
and **I will give you rest**."—**Jesus Christ** (Matthew 11:28)

GOD BLESS YOU AS YOU MAKE THE <ins>RIGHT</ins> <ins>CHOICE</ins>.

The world was **filled** with god & goddess worship. Satan needed them all to come together again into **one world religion**. So he **knitted together** aspects of <u>all</u> religions to create a <u>brand new</u> entity. ***Only 1 thing was different:***

Now it was called "**Christian!**" After **Constantine** started it, making his **sun god** into a **fake "Jesus**," it wasn't hard to make all the **goddesses** into "**visions of Mary**." Then all the *other* gods became saints, angels, etc. ***It was a foolproof system!***

Now all Satan had to do was **connect** the **fake** "**Jesus**," the **sun** & his favorite **wafer** into one. ***Answer: "Jesus" as the wafer god!*** Catholics willingly worshipped a **bread (or child) god** and his **powerful mother!**

It was too good to be true! Pagans were all too willing to worship ***this*** kind of "Christian" god and goddess! And after Satan **finished** his Babylon Religion, the **world** has been willing to **fall down** at the feet of the **pope** & **do his bidding**.

Well, *almost*. Not **everyone** is ready to follow **any** kind of system… *especially* <u>not</u> *Christian Bible-believers!* That's where the Inquisition came in. Rome, that new, spiritual Babylon, is guilty of the blood of <u>*millions*</u> of souls.

But **Jesus** will **judge Babylon Religion**…

AND SHE <u>WILL</u> <u>PAY</u> FOR HER CRIMES!

NOW YOU UNDERSTAND HOW SEMIRAMIS, THAT FAKE BABYLONIAN "GODDESS," BECAME THE ROMAN CATHOLIC "VIRGIN MARY."

WHAT'S THE DIFFERENCE?

The **queen of heaven** is really a **serpent**: she's **beautiful**, but **deadly**. *Flee from her, or she will destroy you!*

"Believe on the **Lord Jesus Christ**, and thou shalt be **saved**"—Acts 16:31

IF YOU HAVE BECOME A <u>CHRISTIAN</u>,
AND ARE <u>STILL</u> IN THIS BABYLON RELIGION,
THE LORD JESUS CHRIST COMMANDS YOU:

Come out of her, my people, that ye be **not partakers** of her **sins**, and that ye **receive not** of her **plagues**.

For **her sins have reached unto heaven**, and **God** hath remembered her **iniquities**. [1]

[1]See Revelation 18:4-5.

OBEY THE LORD JESUS CHRIST. *<u>LEAVE</u> <u>ROME</u>!*
THIS COULD BE YOUR <u>FINAL</u> <u>CALL</u>.

Appendix A:
End Notes

Page 29

Huwawa's head. The entrails made into "Huwawa's face" served as a guide to divination. When an animal was cut up, they used this guide (written on the back of the terracotta (earthenware) figurines of Huwawa (later called by the Assyrians Humbaba or Khumbaba) to determine secrets of the present and future by the way the innards lay. See *Cultural Atlas of Mesopotamia & the Ancient Near East* by Michael Roaf (1990), p. 76, as well as *Mesopotamia: the Invention of the City* by Gwendolyn Leick (2001), illustration #19. For a picture of the whole body of Huwawa, see the *Illustrated Dictionary of Mythology* by Philip Wilkinson (1998), p. 25.

Cedar Forests. For information on the cedar forests of the Zagros mountains, see http://www.kurdistanica.com/english/enviro/ecology.html.

Page 38

Harlot and "Virgin Queen." Many forms of Semiramis were worshipped *both* as a promiscuous woman and as a virgin! For instance, see Hislop's *The Two Babylons* and Turner & Coulter's *Dictionary of Ancient Deities*. Both have very many references to countless goddesses (forms of Semiramis-Ishtar-Inanna) who were worshipped *both* as physically wanton and as virgins. In addition, their worship usually involved prostitutes (see p. 59). These facts are easy to find. Just go to the index and search under the names of goddesses listed in Chapter 3 of this book. (Also see the End Note to p. 59.)

Page 52

Semiramis (Inanna-Ishtar) married Tammuz (Dumuzi). Since she claimed her son was actually her reincarnated husband, she *by definition* had to be "married" to him, whether they actually had a ceremony or not. But we don't have to merely rely on logic. Ancient literature and modern researchers are pretty unanimous (check the books in our Bibliography, for instance) that Inanna (or Ishtar) was married to Tammuz. For a few examples of some ancient literature, see "The Electronic Text Corpus of Sumerian Literature" (online at http://etcsl.orinst.ox.ac.uk/), based at the University of Oxford . Over 350 ancient Sumerian literary works have been both *transliterated* (changed into English letters and phonetic symbols for pronunciation purposes) and *translated* into readable English online. Some of the works that tell about Inanna-Ishtar and Dumuzi (Semiramis and Tammuz) are "Inana's Descent into the Underworld," "Dumuzid and Jectin-Ana," "Dumuzid and His Sisters," "Dumuzid's Dream" and "Inana and Bilulu." And these are just a few of the *thousands* of documents that have been discovered—and just in the Sumerian language. Don't forget that there are also ancient clay writings in Akkadian, Assyrian and Babylonian. There is no shortage of information on the development of Babylon Religion.

Page 53
Ancient myths about Inanna & Dumuzi. See the note to page 52.

Page 55
Tammuz killed by a wild boar. We see this in the myths of Adonis, Attis of Phrygia and Bacchus. See Hislop's *Two Babylons*, pp. 99-101, 273.

Page 59
Cult of Inanna-Ishtar. The cult of Ishtar (or Inanna) flourished over ancient lands, partially owing to its manner of worship – ritual prostitution! They taught that ritual relations with a prostitute were a form of worshipping Ishtar (Semiramis). From these ancient perversions, the concept of "fertility cults" spread all over the world. They linked the fertility of the women to the fruitfulness of the land, and would engage in wild orgies at times, making themselves believe the land would grow good crops because the "gods" would be pleased. For more information on Ishtar and Inanna, see these resources:

- Turner & Coulter's *Dictionary of Ancient Deities* (2000), p. 242.
- *The Once & Future Goddess* by Elinor Gadon (1989), pp. 112, 115 & 118. (But read the warning about this feminist art history book before you read it! See the Annotated Bibliography.)
- Baring & Cashford's, *The Myth of the Goddess: Evolution of an Image* (1991), Chapter 5 and all over the book. (Again, read the warning about this book from an analytical psychology point of view in the Annotated Bibliography.)

Note about the terms "Inanna" and "Ishtar:" The two names are seen as the same person by so many writers that many modern authors simply refer to Semiramis as "Inanna-Ishtar." But in this book we stick mostly to the term "Semiramis" because
  1) People recognize her as the wife of Nimrod
  2) It is the term most used by one of the **best** books on the subject, Alexander Hislop's *The Two Babylons* (1858).

Page 67
Was the sun god "born" on December 25ᵗʰ? Much depends upon the answer to this important question. Sir James George Frazer, whom no one would accuse of being a Christian, wrote a famous book called, *The Golden Bough* (1922). In Chapter 37 he stated his case rather forcefully:

> Indeed the issue of the conflict between the two faiths [Mithraism and what we now call Roman Catholicism] appears for a time to have hung in the balance. An instructive relic of the long struggle is preserved in **our festival of Christmas, which the Church seems to have borrowed directly from its heathen rival.** In the Julian calendar **the twenty-fifth of December was reckoned the winter solstice, and it was regarded as the Nativity of the Sun, because the day begins to lengthen and the power of the sun to increase from that turning-point of the year.**

Page 67, continued

The ritual of the nativity, as it appears to have been celebrated in Syria and Egypt, was remarkable. The celebrants retired into certain inner shrines, from which **at midnight they issued with a loud cry, "The Virgin has brought forth! The light is waxing!" The Egyptians even represented the new-born sun by the image of an infant which on *his birthday, the winter solstice*, they brought forth and exhibited to his worshippers. No doubt the Virgin who thus conceived and bore a son on the twenty-fifth of December was the great Oriental goddess whom the Semites called the Heavenly Virgin or simply the Heavenly Goddess; in Semitic lands she was a form of Astarte.** Now ***Mithra* was regularly identified by his worshippers with *the Sun, the Unconquered Sun, as they called him*; hence *his nativity also fell on the twenty-fifth of December.*** The Gospels say nothing as to the day of Christ's birth, and accordingly the early Church did not celebrate it. In time, however, the Christians of Egypt came to regard the sixth of January as the date of the Nativity, and the custom of commemorating the birth of the Saviour on that day gradually spread until by the fourth century it was universally established in the East. But **at the end of the third or the beginning of the fourth century the Western Church, which had never recognised the sixth of January as the day of the Nativity, adopted the twenty-fifth of December as the true date, and in time its decision was accepted also by the Eastern Church.** (See p. 416. Emphasis mine.)

[It is no coincidence that the Roman religion began to accept the 25th of December around the same time that Constantine became emperor of Rome (312-337 AD)! As emperor, "Pontifex Maximus" *and* "Bishop of Bishops," he wanted to unite the Christians and pagans into one empire. He did this by "Christianizing" pagan holidays, beliefs and gods.[1]]

Was Hislop wrong? Some critics have written that Alexander Hislop, author of *Two Babylons*, cited references that didn't back up what he said. For instance, critics picked at *one* of the citations out of his book, where Hislop showed that December 25th is the birthday of the sun god Horus (Tammuz), not of Jesus. Here's what Hislop wrote:

In Egypt, the son of Isis, the Egyptian title for the queen of heaven, was born at this very time, "about the time of the winter solstice." [2]

But critics have objected that Wilkinson (the author that Hislop cited for his

---

[1] See Daniels, *Did the Catholic Church Give Us the Bible?* (2005), pp. 43-49. Available from Chick Publications.

[2] Hislop, *The Two Babylons*, page 93. The part in quotation marks comes from Sir John Gardner Wilkinson's *A Popular Account of the Ancient Egyptians*, 1836 edition in 5 volumes, Volume 4, page 405.

source) isn't discussing the birth of Isis's son Horus, but a *younger brother* of Horus, named *Harpocrates!* They say Hislop picked the *wrong son of Isis*, someone who is *not the sun god at all!*

Let's check the evidence. "Horus" is Egyptian. But "Harpocrates" is Greek. Greek for *what?* Geoffrey Parrinder, who was[1] one of the top authorities on world religions and Professor of the Comparative Study of Religions in the University of London, wrote the book, *A Dictionary of Non-Christian Religions* (1971). It gives us the answer.

> **Harpocrates.** Greek rendering of Har-pe-khrad, **Horus the Child**, in the popular worship of Ptolemaic Egypt[2] (**see HORUS**). ….
> (See pp. 116-117. Emphasis mine.)

The Dictionary of Ancient Deities (2000) by Patricia Turner & Charles Russell Coulter (published by Oxford University Press), is also very clear.

> **Harpokrates** (Greek)
> Also known as *Harpakhrad, Heru-P-Khart, Heru-Pa-Khret.*
> **A name given to the child Horus by the Greeks,** who looked upon him as the god of silence since he was depicted with his finger to his mouth.
> …. **Sometimes shown as a child, or as a baby on his mother's knee.**
> *See also* **Horus**.
> (See p. 205. Emphasis mine.)

I don't own the *first* edition of Wilkinson's book (usually abbreviated as *Egyptians* and released in five or six volumes). But I do have his *later* edition in *two* volumes. In Volume 2, pp. 52-53, Wilkinson mentions:

> … that Harpocrates, whom they tell us she [Isis] brought forth about the time of the winter tropic …

Wilkinson clearly mentioned Harpocrates. But who did he mean by that? When we *check his own index* under "Harpocrates" it says "*See Horus.*" And under "Horus," it says, "**Horus … the child, or Harpocrates.**" Wilkinson listed the *same reference pages for both Horus and Harpocrates, since they are one and the same god!* So *even Wilkinson's own book* proves that Harpocrates *is* the child Horus. Hislop was right after all.

Hislop's other references. *The Two Babylons* doesn't stop with the mention of the birth of Horus-Harpocrates, however. In Chapter 3 of his book (pp. 91-92), Hislop first showed how the 25th of December could *not* be the birthday of the Lord Jesus Christ . For this he listed numerous references. Then he spent **11 pages** (93-103) piling fact upon fact to prove the so-called "birthday of the sun-

---

[1] Geoffrey Parrinder died on June 16, 2005.
[2] After Alexander the Great died in 323 BC, Egypt was ruled by his general Ptolemy and his descendants until about 30 BC when Cleopatra died and Egypt became part of the Roman Empire. So 323-30 BC is known as the Ptolemaic Period of Egypt.

Page 67, continued

god" was held on December 25th.

These two books alone, *The Golden Bough* and *The Two Babylons*, show us enough facts to convince most skeptics that December 25th was a pagan holiday and birthday of the sun-god, *not* the birthday of our Lord and Saviour Jesus Christ. And the fact remains that Hislop is still an important source of information to this day, partly because he didn't come up with his ideas based on just *one* source or *one* book. He faithfully researched *over 240* (many hard-to-find) sources for his history of Babylon and the Roman Catholic religion. As I have researched these things for myself I have been **astounded** to learn that modern archaeologists, historical linguists, art historians, social scientists and students of ancient history have since *found for themselves* many of the *same* truths Hislop knew over 150 years ago. Hislop was *right!* The critics are *wrong*.

Page 68

Tammuz and the Pagan Calendar. Brandon Staggs, creator of the SwordSearcher Bible software, has compiled an *amazing* array of sources to include in his program. Here's an example of what can be found, using the included search engines. The following are various references to Tammuz on the pagan calendar. (All emphasis is mine). Note all the *different* times of year where Tammuz's death and resurrection are celebrated:

> **From *Easton's Bible Dictionary*, under Tammuz:**
> … a corruption of Dumuzi, the Accadian sun-god (the Adonis of the Greeks), the husband of the goddess Ishtar. **In the Chaldean calendar there was a month set apart in honour of this god, the month of June to July, the beginning of the summer solstice.** At this festival, which lasted six days, the worshippers, with loud lamentations, bewailed the funeral of the god, they sat "weeping for Tammuz" (Ezekiel 8:14).

> **From *Fausset's Bible Dictionary*, under Tammuz:**
> … referring to the river Adonis fed by the melted snows of Lebanon, also to the sun's decreasing heat in **winter**, and to Venus' melting lamentations for Adonis. *Tammuz was the Syrian Adonis* (Jerome), *Venus' paramour, killed by a wild boar*, and according to mythology permitted to spend half the year on earth and obliged to spend the other half in the lower world. **An annual feast was kept to him in June** (Tammuz in the Jewish calendar) at Byblos, when the Syrian women tore off their hair in wild grief, and yielded their persons to prostitution, consecrating the hire of their infamy to Venus; next followed days of rejoicing for his return to the earth. The idea fabled was **spring**'s beauties and the river's waters destroyed by **summer** heat *(*the river Adonis or nahr Ibrahim in **spring** becomes discolored with the heavy rains swelling the streams from Lebanon, which discoloration superstition *attributed to Tammuz' blood*); **or else** the earth clothed with beauty in the half year while the sun is in the upper hemisphere, and

losing it *when he descends to the lower.* [The *Jamieson-Fausset-Brown Commentary* under Ezekiel 8:14 reads basically the same.]

From the *International Standard Bible Encyclopedia* (ISBE), under Tammuz:
(1) … The *Babylonian myth represents Dumuzu, or Tammuz, as a beautiful shepherd slain by a wild boar,* the symbol of **winter.** Ishtar long mourned for him and descended into the underworld to deliver him from the embrace of death (Frazer, Adonis, Attis and Osiris). **This mourning for Tammuz was celebrated in Babylonia by women on the 2nd day of the 4th month,** which thus acquired the name of Tammuz.

The chief seat of the cult in Syria was Gebal (modern Gebail, Greek Bublos) in Phoenicia, to the South of which the river Adonis (Nahr Ibrahim) has its mouth, and its source is the magnificent fountain of Apheca (modern `Afqa), where was the celebrated temple of Venus or Aphrodite, the ruins of which still exist. **The women of Gebal used to repair to this temple in midsummer to celebrate *the death of Adonis or Tammuz*,** and there arose in connection with this celebration those licentious rites which rendered the cult so infamous that it was suppressed by Constantine the Great.

The name *Adonis*, by which this deity was known to the Greeks, is none other than the Phoenician 'Adhon, which is the same in Hebrew. *His death* **is supposed to typify the long, dry summer** of Syria and Palestine, when vegetation perishes, and his return to life the rainy season when the parched earth is revivified and is covered with luxuriant vegetation, **or** his death **symbolizes the cold, rough winter,** *the boar of the myth*, **and his return the verdant spring.**

From *Smith's Bible Dictionary*, under Tammuz:
… A festival in honor of Adonis was celebrated at Byblus in Phoenicia and in most of the Grecian cities, and even by the Jews when they degenerated into idolatry. It took place in **July,** and was accompanied by obscene rites.

From *Albert Barnes' Notes on the Bible*, under Ezekiel 8:14:
… It is not certain that this verse refers to any special act of Tammuz-worship. The month in which the vision was seen, **the sixth month** (**September**), was not the month of the Tammuz-rites. But that such rites had been performed in Jerusalem there can be little doubt. Women are mentioned as employed in the service of idols in Jeremiah 7:18. There is some reason for believing that the weeping of women for Tammuz passed into Syria and Palestine from Babylonia, *Tammuz being identified with Duv-zi, whose loss was lamented by the goddess Istar.* The festival was identical with the Greek "Adoniacs." The worship of Adonis had its headquarters at Byblos, where at certain periods of the

Page 68, continued

year the stream, becoming stained by mountain floods, was popularly said to be red with the blood of Adonis. From Byblos it spread widely over the east and was thence carried to Greece. The contact of Zedekiah with pagan nations (Jeremiah 32:3) may very well have led to the introduction of an idolatry which at this time was especially popular among the eastern nations.

From *Adam Clarke's Commentary on the Bible*, under Ezekiel 8:14: There sat women weeping for Tammuz - This was *Adonis* .... *He is fabled to have been a beautiful youth beloved by Venus, and killed by a wild boar in Mount Lebanon*, whence springs the river Adonis, which was fabled to run blood at his festival in **August**. The women of Phoenicia, Assyria, and Judea worshipped him as dead, with deep lamentation, wearing *priapi* and other obscene images all the while, and they prostituted themselves in honor of this idol. Having for some time mourned him as dead, they then supposed him revivified and broke out into the most extravagant rejoicings.

So as you can see from even these older sources, the pagan calendar gradually added rituals to Tammuz (or Adonis or Dumuzi, etc.) until they largely covered the year.

Pages 70-75
Egypt rewrote the stories and myths from Babylon. The Egyptian priests did not behave like Hollywood directors! But this is meant to illustrate two points:

1. Egypt *rewrote* the myths of Mesopotamia, in some ways *reversing* their meaning. See for instance E.O. James, *The Ancient Gods* (2004), p. 81.
2. The Egyptian form of the myths were *exported* to countries all over the Mediterranean. This is obvious in the most cursory glance at ancient myths.

So after 2300-2200 BC there were *two forms of Mythology* to choose from: Mesopotamian *and* Egyptian.

Page 77
Source for the picture of Anubanini and Ishtar. Although many drawings of Anubanini and Ishtar exist, the one in Edith Porada's *The Art of Ancient Iran: Pre-Islamic Cultures* (1962) is considered authoritative. On p. 40 it shows an 8-pointed star between Anubanini and Ishtar. We have used that depiction to accurately reflect the monument.

Eight-pointed star the symbol of Ishtar. You can find this in many sources. In occultic researcher and Wiccan D.J. Conway's book *Maiden, Mother, Crone* (1994), p. 199, endnote 25, it says:

The symbol of Ashtart was an eight-point star.

In Turner & Coulter's *Dictionary of Ancient Deities* (2000), p. 242 under "Ishtar" it says:

Sometimes she is shown holding her symbol, the eight pointed star.

But the **pentacle**, or **pentagram** (five-pointed star) is *also* the symbol of Ishtar. Conway writes in the glossary of *Maiden, Mother, Crone*, pp. 179:

> **Pentacle, pentagram:** five-point star with one point up; symbol of the Goddess in all Her forms. In ancient Egypt, it was the star of Isis and Nephthys; in the Middle East, that of Ishtar. To the Celts is was the sign of the Morrigan. A sign of the Earth Element in Tarot. … Repulsion of evil; protection.

Page 78

Is Nimrod king of Calneh the same as An god of Nippur? Many researchers are certain that Nippur, 50 miles SE of Babylon, is indeed ancient Calneh.

Over 40,000 written clay tablets have been excavated at Nippur. This is more than almost any other city in the Babylon area. In contrast to Erech (Uruk), Accad (Akkad) and Babylon, Nippur was overthrown quickly. The first time was in the days of Naram-Sin, less than 200 years after it was founded (see p. 77)! Naram-Sin's people rebuilt it (literally in his image) and after that it became largely a city of religious worship. It was not destroyed in later centuries, when other Mesopotamian towns were conquered and demolished. That may be because it was seen as a place of god and goddess worship, not a military threat. But while Dumuzi (Tammuz) and Inanna (Semiramis) can be found in its pantheon (list and order of gods), there is some disagreement as to where Nimrod-Marduk-Sargon fits in. This may be because it is difficult to dig down to the deepest and oldest layers of civilization at Nippur.

There have been many excavations at Nippur, starting in the late 1800s, continuing all the way to the new millennium. But because of the many *layers* of civilization (it was continually occupied all the way to 800 AD), it is difficult to dig to the lowest levels without disturbing the other amazing archaeological finds (known as "artifacts," man-made objects). So even after over 120 years of excavation, only a *part* of Nippur and its vast history have been thoroughly explored. (The fact that it's located in a little country called Iraq might play a small factor in getting American and British archaeologists in as well!) For more information, see "The Nippur Expedition" at the University of Chicago website: http://oi.uchicago.edu/OI/PROJ/NIPI/Nippur.html.

However, there is another explanation. In the beginning, there were only five people who were re-made into gods of one kind or another. That's a pretty limited number. But within a few generations, these few had expanded to literally thousands of different gods and goddesses. So there was a very *limited* period of time when Nippur had only 3-5 gods. After Naram-Sin conquered Calneh (Nippur), he imposed his own ideas very quickly. He changed the names and lists of gods and goddesses, including his own name among them. And soon, with 1) competition among cults, 2) migrations of people who brought their stories of gods (and idols) with them and 3) the need to establish some kind of order in the city, Nippur and other cities developed lists that put the gods and goddesses in some kind of order. Soon there became so many gods and goddesses in those lists that it still takes a trained eye to tell *which* of them are "Nimrod-like" and which are "Tammuz-like."

Michael Roaf is the former director of the British School of Archaeology in Iraq. He is also an associate professor in the Department of Near Eastern Studies at the University of California at Berkeley. He has worked on and/or directed excavation throughout the Near East, and specifically in Bahrain and Iraq. In the section on Nippur in his book, *Cultural Atlas of Mesopotamia and the Ancient Near East* (1990), he tells us his expert opinion about the original order of the gods:

> **The most important goddess was Inanna (or Ishtar)**, with whom most goddesses in later times were identified. She was the goddess of love and of war (the equivalent of the Greek goddesses Aphrodite and Athena combined) and the city goddess of Uruk [Erech] and of Agade [Accad]. **Perhaps originally she had been married to An**, but in later myths **she was the wife of Dumuzi**, who went to the Netherworld in exchange for Inanna. In later times, he was called **Tammuz or Adonis** and was a god who died and revived each year. (See p. 83. Emphasis mine.)

We have already seen how Inanna/Ishtar was *both* the wife of An (Nimrod) *and* the wife of her own son Dumuzi (Tammuz) - who was declared to be the "promised child" (Genesis 3:15) and the reincarnation of Nimrod.

So far we have these three characters at Nippur:

Nimrod	= An
Semiramis	= Inanna-Ishtar
Tammuz	= Dumuzi = Adonis

Anne Baring and Jules Cashford are both members of the International Association of Analytical Psychologists. Baring's interest has been the "underlying unity of Hinduism, Buddhism and Christianity." Cashford's interests have been philosophy and mythology. Both got together and wrote *The Myth of the Goddess: Evolution of an Image* (1991). They believe that the images of God and gods in the Bible, as well as of Mary in Roman Catholicism, are all "evolved" from the ancient goddess and god concepts over countless millennia. So it is interesting to read their perspective in the section on Ashera:

> The goddess **Ashera** was probably the oldest [Canaanite goddess]. As early as 1750 BC **a Sumerian inscription refers to her as the wife of Anu, who can be identified as El**, the father god of the Canaanite pantheon [list of gods], **whose role was closely modeled on that of the Sumerian god An**. (See p. 454. Emphasis mine.)

We know that Nimrod = El. They say El was modeled closely after An. So this links Nimrod with An, as well. They continue:

> **Ashera** was called 'the Lady of the Sea', which **links her to the Sumerian Nammu, and to the Egyptian Isis**, 'born in the all-wetness'. … Her other title was the 'Mother of the Gods', as was **the Sumerian Ninhursag's**, and among her seventy children were **her sons Baal** and Mot [related to the Hebrew for "death"] and her daughter Anath [another goddess made out of Semiramis]. Kings were nourished from her breasts, as they had been by the goddess in Sumeria and Egypt. (See p. 454. Emphasis mine.)

So now we have *more* names for the same characters:

Nimrod	= An = El
Semiramis	= Inanna-Ishtar = Asherah = Nammu = Isis = Ninhursag
Tammuz	= Dumuzi = Adonis = Baal

Just from reading Roaf and Baring & Cashford we see a *lot* of different names for the same gods. But this *appears* to contradict the "pantheon of Sumerian gods" that we find in modern textbooks. Why is this? Because the "pantheon" lists we find in books were written *centuries later and reflect later developments in Babylon Religion.* Always remember that it was much simpler at first: Nimrod, Semiramis, Tammuz, Cush and Shem. There were just **five** characters to work with, *and only one was a woman.*

For a look at the commonly accepted but *later* Sumerian pantheon (list of gods and goddesses in a "family tree" order), see Cotterell & Storm's book, *The Encyclopedia of World Mythology* (1999, 2004), p. 502.

Page 79
The perfectly good and happy god Osiris. Two of the titles given to Osiris (Nimrod) in Egypt were *Wennefer* ("the eternally good being") and *Unnefer* ("he who is continually happy"). See Turner and Coulter's *Dictionary of Ancient Deities* (2000), p. 367 (under "Osiris") and p. 484 (under "Unnefer").

Page 80
Nimrod holding the spotted fawn. Sometimes understanding symbols can be very difficult. Other times it is much easier. In some of the most ancient forms of visual communication, it was quite easy: the picture *was* the symbol. Look at the picture of Nimrod holding the spotted fawn and the branch on page 80. Hold page 80 while you read the next paragraphs.

According to Hans Krause (whose research papers are posted online at www.hanskrause.de) one name for Nimrod in Babylonian-Sumerian is *Gesh-dar*. Each element of that picture on p. 80 has something to do with Nimrod. Many of the objects in that picture were actually represented by the Sumerian symbol-words *gesh* or *dar*. You see, in Sumerian, many words had more than

Page 80, continued

one meaning. (In fact, books I have investigated on ancient Sumerian tell about how translating basic Cuneiform writing can be difficult. Why? Because one single word can stand for **many** different things. The translator has to make a good, educated guess at *which* is being referred to. This is normally easy, but in Sumerian poetry, it can be quite complicated.) Knowing that, it is amazing that the artist **loaded** this drawing of Nimrod with all sorts of **puns** that tell a whole story when read together.

So from *Gesh-dar*:
Gesh means
- Man, hero, mighty one
- High, exalted, lofty
- Branch, which Nimrod is holding in the picture

Dar means
- The headband that Nimrod is wearing, a strip of woven cloth
- Net-skirt, woven fabric or piece of cloth (which Nimrod is also wearing)
- Offspring, or son (remember that Tammuz is supposed to be Nimrod reincarnated/transmigrated – see pp. 41-42)
- The branch Nimrod is holding in the picture has been cut off. "Cut off" or "cut apart" in Sumerian is also *dar*.

Dar also means "spotted one," like the spotted fawn that Nimrod is holding in the picture.

Other things are interesting in this picture.
- Nimrod is holding a horned animal. Horned animal, or a general word for any animal for that matter, in Sumerian is the word *Cush* (Kush). That's the same name as Nimrod's dad!
- The leaves on the branch are said by scholars to be lotus blossoms. Lotus blossoms are a symbol of life from death. Tammuz is supposed to be Nimrod reborn (reincarnated or regenerated or transmigrated).

So the picture speaks of a mighty hero who is cut off, but who is alive from the dead, reincarnated as a child or "son." Krause believes you may also derive that he's the "son of Cush" from the picture. That's a *lot* of imagery. But various researchers believe that's exactly how ancient people wrote and interpreted symbol-pictures (called "symbology"), by drawing and reading these puns in their *alternate* meanings.

Note:
It is amazing that Alexander Hislop, writing years before these ancient writings and languages were discovered or translated, was able to figure out so much of this symbology. He was *years* ahead of his time! And he included it right in the pages of *Two Babylons*. People who argue that Hislop was wrong or made it all

up simply haven't read the newest research on archaeology, linguistics or art history studies. The more I read, the more I find that *supports* Hislop and *refutes* his critics.

Spotted animals later became a symbol of Nimrod.

- *NMR* in Semitic is a word for "leopard," specifically in reference to its spots. (See for instance, Hislop, *Two Babylons*, p. 44; the lexicon for the *Theological Wordbook of the Old Testament* by Harris, Archer and Waltke (1980); and the *Brown, Driver & Briggs Hebrew Lexicon* (1906).
- Greeks saw the spotted fawn as a symbol for Nimrod. The Greek word for Nimrod is *Nebrod* (Greek Νεβρωδ), which means "fawn." This is how the perverted Alexandrian Greek so-called "Septuagint" (abbreviated LXX) spells his name in the four places it occurs (Genesis 10:8-9; 1 Chronicles 1:10 and Micah 5:6). According to the Liddell-Scott Lexicon, the word *nebrodes* means "fawn-like" and it's a term used for Bacchus – whom the Romans called Dionysius.

Nebrod a symbol for Bacchus. The term *nebrod* (spotted fawn) is also a symbol for the god Bacchus himself. When the Greeks saw the Egyptian high priest (called by Wilkinson "the pontiff"), "clad in a leopard skin" (spotted, of course) and then saw the spotted fawn skin nearby, they did a double-take. As Wilkinson put it:

> In this ceremony [the funeral of Osiris at Medinet-Habu], as in some of the tales related of Osiris, we may trace those analogies which led the Greeks to suggest the resemblance between that deity and their Bacchus; as the tambourine, the ivy-bound flower or thyrsus, *and the leopard skin*, which last recalls the leopards that drew his car. *The spotted skin of the nebris, or fawn*, may also be traced in that suspended near Osiris in the region of Amenti. (See *A Popular Account of the Ancient Egyptians in Two Volumes* (1853) Vol. 1, pp. 284-85, as well as pp. 269-70. Emphasis mine.)

To Greeks the spotted fawn and other elements of Osiris' funeral were symbols of Bacchus. And they were right: *Bacchus is a form of Nimrod!*

Page 83

Semiramis is also a moon goddess. According to various authors, all of the following goddesses are, in addition to their other characteristics, also "moon goddesses:" Alilat, Al-Uzzah, Aphrodite, Ariadne, Artemis, Asherah, Astarte, Athena, Cybele, Demeter, Diana, Europa, Hathor, Hecate, Hera, Inanna, Ishtar, Isis, Juno, Lebanah, Neith, Nina, Pasiphae, Penelope, Persephone, Selene & the Aztec Tlazolteotl, among others.

Baring & Cashford take this even further in *The Myth of the Goddess: Evolution of An Image* (1991), p. 302:

Page 83, continued

> **All the Greek goddesses are moon goddesses**: **Persephone** the maiden
> and **Artemis** the virgin personify the new moon, **Demeter** and **Hera**, as
> mother or fulfilled wife, personify the full moon, and **Hecate** of the
> underworld personifies the waning and dark moon. (Emphasis mine.)

How many goddesses can you make from just *one* real woman?
Here are other names for just **one** goddess, *Asherah*, according to Turner &
Coulter's *Dictionary of Ancient Deities* (2000), p. 73 (regrouping mine):

Asherah
> **Among the Akkadians:** Istar
> **Among the Armenians:** Anahit
> **Among the Babylonians:** Ishtar
> **Among the Celts:** Ess-Eorradh
> **Among the Egyptians:** Hathor, Isis
> **Among the Grecians:** Venus
> **Among the Hittites:** Asirat
> **Among the Phoenicians:** Astarte, Ashtoreth
> **Among the Syrians:** Kaukabhta
> **Other names for Asherah:** Achtaroth, Achtoret, Anath-Yahu, Asherat,
> Ashertu, Asirtu, Asratu, Assir, Astar, Astert, Astirati, Astereth, Athrar

These are **25** different names for what these researchers say are the **same exact
goddess!** And these are all made up from *one* form of Semiramis. As Baring &
Cashford say in *The Myth of the Goddess* (p. 254):

> Few goddesses and gods were confined to a single mode of
> manifestation, since they were immanent [present and involved in all of
> nature] divinities and could appear in any context that called them forth.

You can see how easily **thousands** of goddesses can come from the one person
Semiramis. *And that's exactly what happened.*

Page 86
Dogs and black lambs sacrificed to Hecate. See Turner & Coulter's
Dictionary of Ancient Deities (2000), p. 208 under "Hecate."

Goddess of black magic and witchcraft. See Parrinder's *Dictionary of Non-
Christian Religions* (1971), p. 118 and Cotterell & Storm's *Encyclopedia of
World Mythology* (1999, 2004), p. 47. Philip Wilkinson, in his DK *Illustrated
Dictionary of Mythology* (1998), p. 68 calls Hecate the "sorceress and patron of
magicians and witches," and says she "lived in Hades where she presided over
spells and ceremonies." Littleton, *et. al.*, in *Mythology: The Illustrated
Anthology of World Myth & Storytelling* (2002), pp. 135 & 181, simply calls
her a goddess "of witchcraft" or "of ghosts and witchcraft."

Crossroads. Witches, including modern Wiccans, have been especially fond of crossroads. To them they are not only literal road crossings; they are spiritual as well. So while they met at crossroads and did sacrifices, there were *days* and even *hours* they also considered to be "crossroads" between this life and the afterlife. (October 31st at midnight is one of them.) During this time they believed they could communicate with the dead and the "underworld" beings. We know them as *evil spirits* or "*devils*"—and we are expressly forbidden to seek out spirits of any kind! See Leviticus 19:31; 20:6; Deuteronomy 18:10-12; Isaiah 8:19-20 and 1 Timothy 4:1.

Other names for Hecate. The "other names for Hecate" are actually quoted from a Wiccan ritual called "Drawing Down the Moon."

"Drawing Down the Moon." A Wiccan high priestess charges her "children" (fellow Wiccans) with what the goddess expects of them. Then she ultimately "draws down" the moon goddess into herself, which sounds a lot like being possessed with a devil. It is often called "The Charge of the Goddess." See William Schnoebelen's *Wicca: Satan's Little White Lie* (1991), pp. 114, 118-122 & 221, note 11. His quote comes from Stewart Farrar's *What Witches Do* (New York: Coward, MacCann & Geoghegan, 1971), p. 21. See also Margot Adler's *Drawing Down the Moon* (1986), p. 20 as well as *The Grimoire of Lady Sheba* (St. Paul: Llewellyn, 1972), pp. 145-47.

Page 87
The Sacred Stone of the goddess Astarte. This illustration is made to look like the so-called "sacred stone" as it is being excavated. For more ancient illustrations of the "sacred stone of the moon goddess," see M. Esther Harding's *Woman's Mysteries: Ancient & Modern* (1971), p. 40.

Human sacrifices to pagan gods & goddesses. It hardly seems necessary to prove humans were sacrificed to gods and goddesses. But for more information about pagan sacrifices, including archaeological details of sacrifices to Baal and Moloch, see Nigel Davies' *Human Sacrifice: In History and Today* (1981). (See the Bibliography for more information.)

Page 88
Tlazolteotl (Also spelled Tlazolteutl). She is actually a goddess of much more than we list on p. 88. Turner & Coulter (2000, p. 470) say she is a:

> Moon Goddess. Earth Goddess. Goddess of Excrement. Goddess of purification and curing. Goddess of Love and Fertility. Goddess of Childbirth. Lifegiver. Forgiver of sins. Goddess of Sexual Pleasure. Patron of Gambling. Great Spinner of Thread and Weaver of the Fabric of Life. One of the nine Lords of the Night Hours. … **She is the power behind all magic in the Aztec world.** (Emphasis mine.)

She also literally "heard confession!" Again from Turner & Coulter:

> Once in a lifetime, confession could be given to a priest. This act was

Page 88, continued

usually delayed until it was thought that age would nullify temptation. The "sinner" would appear before the priest and list all mis-deeds. Wrong-doing would include disobeying the gods, deviating from the mores of the community, cowardice during battle, and neglect of sacrifices. Offerings were made to the gods, and absolution was granted by Tlazolteutl's priest. If the confession was honest, Tlazolteutl would absorb the sins of the confessor, and purify the soul.

Note about Tlazolteotl on the broomstick. This illustration, while faithful to actual drawings of this goddess, has been "cleaned up." You see, according to Turner & Coulter (2000, p. 470):

As Tlazolteutl **she appears nude,** riding on a broom. She wears a horned headdress with a crescent moon and she holds a red snake. She also has a crescent moon decoration on her nose. … **Tlazolteutl represents the planet Venus. She is often depicted wearing a flayed human skin** …. (Emphasis mine.)

In D.J. Conway's *Maiden, Mother, Crone* (1994, pp. 99-100) she is drawn in another version, as an old woman, clothed, without the snake and a very different hat. She adds these elements to Tlazolteotl's description:

Tlazolteotl of the Aztecs, whose name can be translated as "lady of filth" or "dirty lady," rode a broomstick through the night skies, wore a peaked hat, **and was associated with the Moon, the snake, and the bat. Like Hecate, much of Her worship was performed at crossroads.** The Ciuateteo (right honorable mothers) were Her priestesses; they were said to fly through the air … and were connected with childbirth. **Tlazolteotl was connected with Witchcraft, sexuality, gambling, temptation and black magick.** (Emphasis mine.)

Tlazolteotl, alias Coatlicue. Littleton, editor of *The Illustrated Anthology of World Myth & Storytelling* (2002, pp. 550-51, 577) reveals even more information about this gross goddess:

One of the nastier Aztec customs took place in her name. Young girls might be forced into prostitution in the barracks for trainee warriors, only to be ceremonially killed once their career had reached an end, their bodies dumped as polluted refuse in the marshes of Lake Texcoco [near modern Mexico City].

Coatlicue, the fertile virgin. As the goddess **Coatlicue (co-AT-li-KWAY)**, She was both *fertile* and considered a *virgin* at the same time! The book says, "This led certain Catholic commentators to associate this aspect of Coatlicue with the Virgin Mary." - *Believe it or not!*

Page 92
Hathor, the "house" or "womb" of Horus. See D.J. Conway, *Maiden,*

Mother, Crone (1994), pp. 56-57. Also see Baring & Cashford, *The Myth of the Goddess* (1991), p. 252; Turner & Coulter, *Dictionary of Ancient Deities* (2000), p. 206; and E.O. James, *The Ancient Gods* (2004), p. 82.

Page 96
Sacrificing to idols is sacrificing to devils. These verses say it well:

> **Deuteronomy 32:16-17** [16] They provoked him to jealousy with **strange gods, with** abominations provoked they him to anger. [17] They sacrificed unto **devils**, not to God; to **gods whom they knew not,** to **new gods that came newly up,** whom your fathers feared not.

> **Psalm 106:36-38** [36] And they served their **idols**:which were a snare unto them. [37] Yea, they sacrificed their sons and their daughters unto **devils,** [38] And shed innocent blood, *even* the blood of their sons and their daughters, whom they sacrificed unto the **idols of Canaan**: and the land was polluted with blood.

> **1 Corinthians 10:19-21** [19] What say I then? that the **idol** is any thing, or that which is offered in sacrifice to **idols** is any thing? [20] But I *say*, that the things which the Gentiles sacrifice, they sacrifice to **devils**, and not to God: and I would not that ye should have fellowship with **devils**. [21] Ye cannot drink the cup of the Lord, and the **cup of devils**: ye cannot be partakers of the Lord's table, and of the **table of devils**.

> **Revelation 9:20** And the rest of the men which were not killed by these plagues yet repented not of **the works of their hands**, that they should not worship **devils**, and **idols of gold, and silver, and brass, and stone, and of wood: which neither can see, nor hear, nor walk:**

So remember this: behind every idol, image or statue of a "god" is a **devil**.

Page 97
Eating the wafer god Osiris. Anti-Christian, Bible-*dis*believer T.W. Doane wrote the book, *Bible Myths & Their Parallels in Other Religions* (1882) to document his years of research on the pagan origins of so-called "Christian" belief and practice. Here is an excerpt from his book about eating the "wafer god" Osiris, supported by four separate sources:

> The ancient *Egyptians*—as we have seen—annually celebrated the *Resurrection* of their God and Saviour *Osiris*, at which time they commemorated his death by the *Eucharist*, eating the sacred cake, or wafer, *after it had been consecrated by the priest, and become veritable flesh of his flesh*. The bread, after sacerdotal rites, became mystically the body of *Osiris*, and, in such a manner, *they ate their god*. Bread and wine were brought to the temples by the worshippers, as offerings.

> The *Therapeutes* or *Essenes*, whom we believe to be of Buddhist origin, and who lived in large numbers in Egypt, also had the ceremony of the

sacrament among them. Most of them, however, being temperate, substituted water for wine, while other drank a mixture of water and wine.

Pythagoras, the celebrated Grecian philosopher, who was born about the year 570 B.C., performed this ceremony of the *sacrament*. He is supposed to have visited Egypt, and there availed himself of all such mysterious lore as the priests could be induced to impart. He and his followers practiced asceticism, and peculiarities of diet and clothing, similar to the Essenes …. (p. 306)

Eating the "cereal deity." Another non-Christian, Sir James George Frazer, wrote *The Golden Bough: A Study in Magic & Religion* (1922), which *TIME* Magazine labeled, "one of the 20th century's most influential books." Frazer's non-Christian book devotes chapter 50 to the concept of "Eating the God." In it he describes the Aino of Japan and their devotion to millet, "the divine cereal," or "**the cereal deity**":

> … **they pray to and worship him before they will eat of the cakes made from the new millet**. And even where the **indwelling divinity of the first fruits** is not expressly affirmed, it appears to be implied both by the solemn preparations made for eating them and by the danger supposed to be incurred by persons who venture to partake of them without observing the prescribed ritual. In all such cases, accordingly, we may not improperly describe the **eating of the new fruits as a sacrament or communion with a deity**, or all events with a powerful spirit. (See p. 565. Emphasis mine.)

In other words, when the Aino of Japan ate the cakes of cereal (grain), they believed they were eating their god!

Eating the god made of dough. Frazer later told of elaborate ceremonies performed by the Aztecs centuries before Spaniards and their Catholicism came to Mexico. In one, twice a year (in May and December) they made an image of their sun god Huitzilopochtli (WHIT-sil-oh-POHKT-lee), also called Vitzilipuztli (VIT-sil-i-POOST-lee), out of dough and broke it in pieces, which were "solemnly eaten by his worshippers." (p. 566). After he listed other bread-god ceremonies, he stated:

> From this interesting passage we learn that **the ancient Mexicans**, even before the arrival of Christian missionaries, **were fully acquainted with the doctrine of transubstantiation** [bread being turned magically into a god] and acted upon it in the solemn rites of their religion. **They believed that by consecrating bread their priests could turn it into the very body of their god**, so that all who thereupon partook of the consecrated bread entered into **a mystic communion with the deity by**

receiving a portion of his divine substance into themselves. (See p. 568. Emphasis mine.)

Another similar ceremony, **performed by the Aztecs during the winter solstice in December,** involved making a dough-image of their god and shooting flint-tipped darts at it.. It was called, "killing the god Huitzilopochtli so that his body might be eaten." After the "heart" and other parts were divided, all the males ate of this "communion." This was called *teoqualo*, "god is eaten." (See pp. 568-9. Emphasis mine.)

It is interesting that according to Turner & Coulter's *Dictionary of Ancient Deities*, pp. 226-227, Huitzilopochtli is the Aztec's chief god, their **sun god, storm god, god of lightning** [all of which sound like Baal/Tammuz] and the **son of Coatlicue!** In the End Note for page 89, we have seen that Coatlicue was likened to the Roman Catholic "Virgin Mary." Now we see that Huitzilopochtli is her child. Listen to the description by Turner & Coulter:

> Huitzilopochtli ... led his people on an arduous journey ... from Aztlan [the Aztecs' legendary island home] to Coatepec (Hill of the Serpent). It was here that **he was reborn.** Huitzilopochtli's **mother Coatlicue** was sweeping the temple one day when she tucked feathers into her blouse. When she finished her task and went to remove the feathers, they were gone. **She knew she was pregnant. This divine impregnation was the god's beginning of his rebirth.** ... **Other depictions show him** with hummingbird feathers on his left, **holding a stick shaped like a snake.** ... **Human sacrifices were frequently made to Huitzilopochtli** (See pp. 226-27. Emphasis mine.)

These gods look very familiar:

Semiramis	**= Coatlicue = Tlazolteotl (black magic goddess) = Hecate**
Tammuz	**= Huitzilopochtli = Baal = Adonis = Attis = Horus**

Coatlicue was said to look *suspiciously like* the Catholic "Virgin Mary." Huitzilopochtli looks *awfully similar* to the Catholic wafer god called "Jesus."

No wonder Catholicism was so readily accepted in Mexico!

Page 114

God's prophetic clock. This can get complicated, so I will attempt to make it as simple to understand as possible.

1. For some reason, God counts years as **360 days**, not 365 1/4 days. Compare these parallel statements:

> **Time, times and half a time** (Daniel 12:7 & Revelation 12:14)
> **1,260 days** (Revelation 11:3 & 12:6)
> **42 months** (Revelation 11:2 & 23:5)

Page 114, continued

All three equal 3 1/2 years, *if* the years are 360 days long. Otherwise God would have had to say "1,278.375 days," not the simple 1,260.

2. Just as the word "time" meant "year" above, the word "week" in Daniel 9 means "7 years." And just as we saw in #1 above, a year is 360 days. So we have to make a conversion between 365 1/4 and 360-day years in order to understand what the Hebrews (and even the Devil himself) already knew:

> **Seventy weeks** (Daniel 9:24) = 490 years of 360 days = 176,400 days
> **Sixty nine weeks** (Daniel 9:25) = 483 years of 360 days = 173,880 days
> **173,880 days** = 476 years, 21 days in our Gregorian 365 1/4 day years.

3. So from "the going forth of the commandment to restore and to build Jerusalem unto Messiah the Prince" shall be 476 years and 3 weeks. While Cyrus was anointed by God to begin the return of captives to Israel, it was the decree of Artaxerxes in about 445 BC (see Nehemiah 2) that permission was granted to "build" Jerusalem back up (Nehemiah 2:5).

4. 445 BC plus 476 years (plus 1, because there is no year "Zero" to count in the Gregorian calendar) = approximately 31 AD. Given a normal lifespan, that showed Satan (and anyone who took the time to read carefully) that Messiah had to be born sometime around the days of Herod the Great (somewhere between about 20 and 2 BC).

There! That wasn't so hard, was it?

Page 115
Babylon literally fell apart, one piece at a time. 539 BC, when Belshazzar saw "the writing on the wall" (Daniel 5), was the beginning of the end for the Babylonian Empire. Note the following chart:

- **539 BC**— *"Mene, Mene, Tekel, Upharsin"* "Numbered, Numbered, Weighed and Divided." God showed Daniel that Babylon was "weighed in the balances and found wanting," and was to be "divided" among the Medes and the Persians (Daniel chapter 5). *That very night* Cyrus the Great captured Babylon!
- **522/21 BC**—Babylon captured by Darius. Babylon's famous 100 gates guarding the city were torn down.
- **482 BC**—Babylon captured by Xerxes. Whole sections of the city were ransacked and left to ruin. Then Babylon was lumped in with Assyria and put under heavy taxation.
- **331 BC**—Alexander the Great tried to restore Babylon. But he died there and the project was abandoned.
- **307-300 BC**—Many citizens of Babylon left to colonize the new city of Seleucia, about 90 miles away.
- **160-140 BC**—Babylon captured by rival armies four times, the fourth

time by King Mithridates I of Parthia, ending Greek rule.
- **130 BC**—Babylon captured by Antiochus VII Sidetes.
- **127/26 BC**—Babylon captured by Hyspaosines.
- **126-123**—Babylon's marketplace and some of its temples burnt by Himeros. Most of the city was destroyed. Many remaining citizens sent as slaves to Media.
- **122 BC**—Babylon recaptured by King Mithridates I of Parthia.
- **30 BC**—By the time of the Greek geographer Strabo (63 BC-19AD) Babylon was "in great part deserted."

In short, while Babylon still had a small colony of settlers, after Cyrus the Great it ceased to be a world power. Eventually the city was covered up in the sands of history, never to be built again.

Note: While Saddam Hussein, former ruler of Iraq (1979-2003) claimed to be "rebuilding Babylon," all he really did was stick up a façade that resembled a desert tourist trap. The City of Babylon itself was *never* rebuilt, as God promised in Jeremiah 51.

Page 126
Jesus' birth less than 9 months after Joseph wed Mary. According to Luke 1:26 & 36, six months into Elizabeth's pregnancy with John the Baptist the angel Gabriel appeared to Mary. And after she humbly declared, "Behold, the handmaiden of the Lord; be it unto me according to thy word" (Luke 1:38), the Holy Ghost came upon her and placed the Son of God, God the Son, Jesus Christ, into her womb (Luke 1:30-35; 42-43 & Matthew 1:18). Then "in those days" she arose and went "with haste" to see her cousin Elizabeth. When Joseph found out she was pregnant, his first thought was to "put her away privily." Betrothal was considered so binding in those days that it literally took a divorce to cancel the wedding! But God reassured Joseph (Matthew 1:19-21) and he married her. He didn't consummate the marriage until she bore the Lord Jesus (Matthew 1:24-25) and they *together* bore James, Joses, Simon and Judas (see p. 122). So they married sometime *after* God put Jesus inside her womb.

A statement in the Gospels may imply that others knew the *timing* of his birth.

In John 8, Jesus contrasted His own works that please His Father to that of the Pharisees, who claimed Abraham as their father. At one point Jesus began to confront them directly:

> Ye do the deeds of your father. Then said they to him, We be not born of fornication; we have one Father, *even* God. (John 8:41)

Some say that the words, "We be not born of fornication" are another way of saying, "We know who *our* father is!" with a double-meaning: to accuse Jesus of being an illegitimate child. But the Lord Jesus is the Son of God the Father (John 8:42), and clearly replied, "Ye are of *your* father the *devil*" (John 8:44).

Page 126, continued

Unlike Semiramis, this was no unplanned pregnancy. It was *prophesied!*
- **Genesis 49:10** says Shiloh (literally "the One to whom it belongs") shall come from the tribe of Judah. **Isaiah 11:1, 10; Jeremiah 23:5 & 33:15** say the "branch" shall come from the line of Jesse and David. Jesus **is** from the tribe of Judah through David, by both Joseph (legally) and Mary. (See **Matthew 1 & Luke 3:23-38**)
- **Isaiah 7:14** says He will be born of a virgin. He was! (**Luke 1:27**)
- **Micah 5:2** says He will be born in Bethlehem. He was! (**Matthew 2:1, 5, 6, 8, 16 & Luke 2:4 & 15**) Most people did not know that little fact. They only knew He was from Nazareth in Galilee. (See **Matthew 21:10-11 & John 7:40-52**)

The Lord Jesus showed He was God come in the flesh. Unbelieving leaders claimed He was just an illegitimate child. Jesus proved who He was: He healed the sick, cast out devils, cleansed the lepers, raised the dead, and Himself rose from the dead, before *many witnesses*.

Tammuz couldn't do *any* of that. He was just an illegitimate child.

Page 129
About the "Great Hallel." The Babylonian Talmud, Volume 4, Bavli Pesahim, (Folios 99B – 121B), 10:7, Section II, 12A-G reveals these interesting facts about the "Hallel:"

    A. *Now that there is the great Hallel, how come we recite this one* [this particular "Hallel," consisting of Psalms 113-118]?

    B. It is because **it contains these five references**: the exodus from Egypt, dividing the Reed Sea, giving of the Torah, **resurrection of the dead**, and **the anguish of the Messiah.**

    C. The exodus from Egypt: "When Israel came forth out of Egypt" (Psalm 114:1);

    D. dividing the Reed [Red] Sea: "the sea saw it and fled" (Psalm 114: 3);

    E. giving of the Torah: "the mountains skipped like rams" (Psalm 114: 4);

    F. **resurrection of the dead: "I shall walk before the Lord in the land of the living" (Psalm 116: 9);**

    G. and **the anguish of the Messiah: "not to us, Lord, not to us" (Psalm 115: 1)**

Also note that when Jesus rode the donkey through the streets of Jerusalem, the people cried, "Hosanna!" which is a cry to God, asking Him, "Save now!" They fully expected the Kingdom of God to appear as Jesus came to become the Messiah and the true King of Israel! The Romans would now be defeated!

They were about to be terribly disappointed.

Page 151
Christians killed for sport on hill Vaticanus. They were actually killed near the *very obelisk* that stands before the Vatican today! See Peter Tomkins, *The Magic of Obelisks* (1981), p. 10.

Page 154
The "Missing Verses" of Mark (16:9-20). That is not a *drawing*; it is an *actual scanned picture* of Codex Vaticanus! Huge, ancient books (called "codices"—singular "codex") were expensive. They had to be made by hand, and space was at a premium. In modern Bibles, when a book of the Bible ends, the new book starts on the next page. Not so in Alexandria! When they finished a book of the New Testament, they wrote a summary title for that book to remind the readers what they just read. Then they began the next book *starting in the very next column!* I have verified this myself in scanned copies of Codex Vaticanus and Sinaiticus New Testaments (see *Figure 1*, for example). This is true every time—*except* in **Codex Vaticanus** at **Mark 16!** Look back at page 154. There is an *empty column* where either verses 9-20 should be, or else the next book (Luke) should have begun. Why is it empty? *I think you know.*

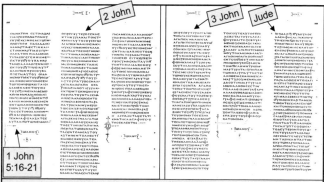

Figure 1. Two successive pages out of Codex Vaticanus. Note how the next book of the Bible follows *in the very next column.* Now look back at Mark 16 (p. 154). The column that *should* have 16:9-20 is *left blank!* As anyone can see, **something is clearly missing!**

For more information on Mark 16:9-20 and why it belongs in the Bible, see Daniels, *Answers to your Bible Version Questions* (2003), pp. 117-119.

Page 155
Mithras = *Sol Invictus*, "the Unconquered Sun" = Tammuz. The late E.O. James (1888-1972), in *The Ancient Gods: The History & Diffusion of Religion in the Ancient Near East & the Eastern Mediterranean* (2004 edition of a 1960 book—see the Annotated Bibliography) put it this way:

Page 155, continued

> **Mithras** in his original Indo-European form was the Vedic god of light, **Mitra**, and subsequently ... was identified with *Sol Invictus*, **'the invincible sun,'** having been equated with the Babylonian solar deity **Shamash** and the Hellenic **Helios.**
> (See p. 318. Emphasis mine).

Apollo is the Greek equivalent to Babylonian **Shamash** and the Egyptian **Horus.** (For instance, see Turner & Coulter's *Dictionary of Ancient Deities* (2000) under "Apollo," p. 62.)

Can anyone guess the **birthday of Mitra**? Again from Turner & Coulter:

"His birthday is December 25," [1] *just like Tammuz*. So to sum up:

> **Tammuz as the *sun god* = Mithras = Mitra = *Sol Invictus* = Shamash = Helios = Apollo = Horus, etc.**

And the list of synonyms for these gods keeps getting bigger and bigger.

Page 156
The cross as a pre-Christian symbol. See T.W. Doane, *Bible Myths & Their Parallels in Other Religions* (1882), Chapter 33, pp. 339-351. In these pages, he demonstrates a few startling facts:

Pagans have erected crosses at various sites centuries before Christ:
- Buddhists, who also put "the sign of the cross" on the heads of followers;
- Egyptians, who used what we call the "Calvary cross;" a cross rising out of a heart as the hieroglyph of goodness; and a cross on their "sacred cakes," just like Catholics do on "Good Friday;"
- Babylonians, who had the cross as the sign of the gods An and Bal;
- Persians, who had it as their ensign when warring with Alexander the Great;
- Phoenicians, who used it on their own version of a rosary;
- Even Greeks and Romans used the "Calvary cross" for centuries.

The "*chi-rho*" was actually the "monogram of Osiris" and of "Jupiter Ammon!" He verified this with numerous sources, which he clearly listed in his bibliography. *Check it for yourself!*

IHS This symbol, in whatever language or form (usually Greek or Roman) was used by pagans as well. It was originally a monogram of Bacchus! People of many religions, from the Maharajah of Cashmere to the Jesuits, adapted and slightly respelled it, giving it their own meanings, until Bacchus' symbol became the "IHS" on catholic wafer gods today.

---

[1] See Turner & Coulter's *Dictionary of Ancient Deities* (2000), p. 325, under "Mitra."

Page 176

Fatima as 2nd in heaven, next to Mary. Muhammad described Fatima's place in heaven shortly before his death. In the *Hadith* of Sahih Bukhari, Volume 4, Book 56, #819, 'Aisha (one of his many wives) narrated:

> Once Fatima came walking and her gait resembled the gait of the Prophet. The Prophet said, "Welcome, O my daughter!" Then he made her sit on his right or on his left side, and then he told her a secret and she started weeping. I asked her, "Why are you weeping?" He again told her a secret and she started laughing. I said, "I never saw happiness so near to sadness as I saw today." I asked her what the Prophet had told her. She said, "I would never disclose the secret of Allah's Apostle." When the Prophet died, I asked her about it. She replied. "The Prophet said, 'Every year Gabriel used to revise the Qur'an with me once only, but this year he has done so twice. I think this portends my death, and you will be the first of my family to follow me.' So I started weeping. **Then he said. 'Don't you like to be the mistress of all the ladies of Paradise or the mistress of all the lady believers?** So I laughed for that."

Page 177

Full quotes on Mary and the Muslims. It is *very* difficult to fit complete quotes into small spaces! So to give you the context, here they are in full.

The following is the full quote of Mary of Agreda.

> In the last times the Lord will especially spread the renown of His Mother. Mary began salvation, and by her intercession it will be concluded. Before the Second Coming of Christ, Mary must, more than ever, shine in mercy, might and grace in order to bring unbelievers into the Catholic Faith. The powers of Mary in the last times over the demons will be very conspicuous. Mary will extend the reign of Christ over the heathens and Mohammedans and it will be a time of great joy when Mary, as Mistress and Queen of Hearts, is enthroned.

The following is a fuller quote of Fulton J. Sheen:

> It is our firm belief that the fears some entertain concerning the Muslims are not to be realized, but that Muslimism, instead, will eventually be converted to Christianity--and in a way that even some of our missionaries never suspect. It is our belief that this will happen not through the direct teachings of Christianity, but through a summoning of the Muslims to a veneration of the Mother of God.

Appendix B:
Annotated Bibliography

Note on terms:
Illustrated: Anything from a few pictures on a single page, up to many pictures interspersed throughout the book.
Thoroughly illustrated: Full of helpful pictures to aid in understanding.

Adler, Margot. *Drawing Down the Moon: Witches, Druids, Goddess-Worshippers, & Other Pagans in America Today.* Revised and expanded edition. New York: Penguin books, 1986. This is a thoroughly anti-Christian, paganism-promoting book. It is useful for understanding the neo-Pagan movement, but it tries to suck the reader into paganism. Illustrated.

Baring, Anne & Cashford, Jules. *The Myth of the Goddess: Evolution of an Image.* New York: Penguin Books, 1991. Baring & Cashford claim that goddess worship supposedly "evolved" from primitive people 20,000 years ago, all the way to modern Mary worship as the new "mother goddess." They refer a lot to Jungian psychology, which teaches there is an underlying "universal unconscious" in all humans. And this is understandable: both are members of the International Association of analytical Psychologists! Baring believes in the "underlying unity of Hinduism, Buddhism and Christianity," and Cashford teaches mythology. A goddess-worshipping book, not Christian by any means. Illustrated.

Belán, Kyra. *The Virgin in Art: From Medieval to Modern.* New York: Barnes & Noble Books (by arrangement with Parkstone Press Ltd.), 2005. Artist Dr. Belán, shows, in a number of representative paintings, how the Roman Catholic Mary was made into a newer version of ancient goddesses. She picks out the many plain clues left by the artists that turned pagan goddess worshippers into Catholic Mary worshippers. Her descriptions are very interesting. She may be Catholic—but definitely not a Christian. Thoroughly illustrated.

Caner, Ergun & Caner, Emir. *Unveiling Islam: An Insider's Look at Muslim Life & Beliefs.* Grand Rapids, Michigan: Kregel Publications, 2002. This Gold Medallion Book Award winner deserves its excellent reputation. It is sensitive, it is revealing & it is a way of seeing Islam from the inside out. It is also a way of seeing how the gospel of Jesus Christ can penetrate a Muslim's heart.

Carroll, James. *Constantine's Sword: The Church & the Jews. A History.* New York: Houghton Mifflin Co., 2001. Carroll, a former Catholic priest (ordained 1969), spent years trying to make sense of the relationship between the Vatican and the Jewish people—and other non-Catholics, as well. His conclusions are colored by his Catholicism, but his citations of history are generally pretty accurate. He also records some important incidents in Constantine's life.

Conway, Deanna J. *Maiden, Mother, Crone: The Myth & Reality of the Triple Goddess.* St. Paul, MN: Llewellyn Publications, 2003. D.J. Conway is a New Age and Occult researcher who has studied Yogananda, "Qabala, healing, herbs and Wicca" and is an ordained minister in two New Age churches. She says her "heart lies within the Pagan cultures." She believes that the "goddess," or "divine creative force," lies within and actually tries to get the reader to worship the "goddess" in her three main forms: maiden, mother and crone. She includes not only principles and mythological history, but also meditations and actual rituals to worship the "goddess." She describes some goddess myths better than I have found in many other books. Totally anti-Christian. Illustrated.

Cotterell, Arthur & Storm, Rachel. *The Encyclopedia of World Mythology: A Comprehensive A-Z of the Myths & Legends of Greece, Rome, Egypt, Persia, India, China, & the Norse & Celtic Lands.* London: Lorenz Books (an imprint of Annes Publishing Ltd.), 1999, 2004. This is a fairly accurate book, well-illustrated. Gives at least one perspective of each mythological character it describes. A good supplementary research book. Non-Christian, but not anti-Christian. Thoroughly illustrated.

Daniels, David W. *Answers to Your Bible Version Questions.* Ontario: Chick Publications, 2003. Answers 60 questions people ask about Bible versions. Includes an annotated bibliography, subject & Scripture indexes.

Daniels, David W. *Did the Catholic Church Give Us the Bible? The True History of God's Words.* Ontario: Chick Publications, 2005. This book shows the *two* histories of the Bible: one of God preserving His words through His people; the other of the Devil using the Roman Catholic religion to pervert God's words through her "scholars." Thoroughly illustrated by Jack Chick.

Davies, Nigel. *Human Sacrifice: In History and Today.* New York: William Morrow & Co., Inc, 1981. Dr. Davies (1920-2004) was one of the most famous Latin American archaeologists. Raised in England, Davies received his Ph.D. at the Universidad Autonoma de Mexico and became an expert in pre-Columbian Mexican civilizations. He wrongly assumed Christianity arose from the same pagan origins as other religions. Non-Christian, not anti-Christian. Illustrated.

Dalley, Stephanie, Editor & Translator. *Myths from Mesopotamia: Creation, the Flood, Gilgamesh & Others.* New York: Oxford University Press, 1989. Revised Edition, 2000. This book is a translation of many of the famous epic stories that were written in cuneiform (wedge-writing) on clay tablets that were discovered in the 1800s-1900s. Illustrated.

Doane, T.W. *Bible Myths & Their Parallels in Other Religions, Being a Comparison of the Old & New Testament Myths & Miracles with Those of Heathen Nations of Antiquity Considering also Their Origin & Meaning.* New York: The Truth Seeker Company, 1882. Reprinted by Kessinger Publishing's Rare Mystical Imprints (www.kessinger.net). This anti-Christian book seeks to discredit Christianity by comparing historical Bible stories with various myths of ancient religions. Ignores the facts when the Bible story happened **first**, then the pagans adapted the Bible story into their mythology. Illustrated.

Frazer, Sir James George. *The Golden Bough: A Study in Magic and Religion.* 1 Volume Abridged Edition. New York: Touchstone (Simon & Schuster), 1996. Originally published in 1922 by Macmillan, Inc. This is a book loved by anti-Christians, who say that Christianity evolved just like any other pagan religion, and who ignore the differences between Bible Christianity and Roman Catholic religion. 827 pages of small-print text. Still very informative.

Gadon, Elinor W. *The Once & Future Goddess.* New York: HarperCollins, 1989. Gadon is an art historian who specializes in Indian art & culture and in analysis of images and symbols in the context of their culture. She believes that the "goddess," in whatever form she takes through history, is the key to healing and transforming the world. She believes the "goddess" has "reemerged" in society to bring about a "new consciousness" of love, freedom and self-awareness that does not exist in any male-dominated religion (which for her includes Christianity). Illustrated.

Gahlin, Lucia. *Egyptian Religion: The Beliefs of Ancient Egypt Explored and Explained.* London: Anness Publishing Ltd., 2002. This book focuses on six topics: Burial Sites, Funerary Religion, Tombs, Popular Religion, Temples & Priests and Akhenaten's Religious Revolution. Thoroughly illustrated.

Grant, Michael. *Constantine the Great: The Man & His Times.* New York: Barnes & Noble Books (by arrangement with Scribner, an imprint of Simon & Schuster, Inc.), 1993. This book makes Constantine out to be a Christian who needed to change his empire slowly. I disagree that he was any kind of Bible Christian. But there are still many excellent snippets of history available here where you can verify for yourself what kind of man he was. Illustrated.

Harding, M. Esther. *Woman's Mysteries: Ancient and Modern. A Psychological Interpretation of the Feminine Principle as Portrayed in Myth, Story, and Dreams.* New York: G.P. Putnam's Sons for the C.G. Jung Foundation for Analytical Psychology, 1971. This book, originally published in 1935, contains an introduction by Carl Jung himself. Harding was trained *by* Dr. Jung in the 1920s and remained a practicing Jungian analyst until she died in May 1971. This book is cited specifically because it openly admits there is evidence of human sacrifices to Astarte, Diana and countless other names for Semiramis. Non-Christian. Illustrated.

Hislop, Alexander. *The Two Babylons: Or, The Papal Worship Proved to Be the Worship of Nimrod & His Wife.* Ontario, California: Chick Publications. Reprint of the original 1858 book. This is *the* classic book to show how modern Roman Catholicism is the same religion as that of ancient Babylon. It is so powerful in its message that the Devil has been trying to discredit it, especially since the late 1990s. It is amazingly accurate, written before archaeology became what is today. Very detailed. Can be confusing at times. Illustrated.

James, E. O. *The Ancient Gods: The History and Diffusion of Religion in the Ancient Near East and the Eastern Mediterranean.* Edison, NJ: Castle Books, 2004. Originally published in 1960 in Great Britain by Weidenfeld & Nicolson. Late Professor James (1888-1972) was Professor Emeritus of the History & Philosophy of Religion at the University of London after a long and distinguished career & holding many other teaching positions. His book tries to show how gods and goddesses and their cults were linked with "nature, agriculture and the seasons, fertility, and the preoccupation with life and death and the struggle for existence" (from the front flap). This anthropologist, like many others, believed in the idea that religions such as Christianity "evolved" from "primitive" nature religion. Non-Christian. Illustrated.

Leick, Gwendolyn. *Mesopotamia: The Invention of the City.* New York: Penguin Books, 2001. Leick is an anthropologist and Assyriologist who lectures at the American International University in London and in Design Theory at Chelsea College of Art and Design. She also lectures on history, archaeology and anthropology of the Middle East and writes about the Ancient Near East. This book describes her view of the creation and "life" of ten cities: Eridu, Uruk, Shuruppak, Akkad, Ur, Nippur, Sippar, Ashur, Nineveh and Babylon. Illustrated.

Lings, Martin. *Muhammad: His Life Based on the Earliest Sources.* Rochester, Vermont: Inner Traditions International, 1983. Lings served as Keeper of the Oriental Manuscripts at the British Museum, was consultant to the World of Islam Festival Trust and in 1977 participated in the Conference on Islamic Education in Mecca. He has written for *Studies in Comparative Religion, The New Encyclopaedia of Islam* & *Encyclopaedia Brittanica.* In short, his fresh translation of 8th & 9th century Arabic sources is *very* authoritative to Muslim scholars. It also documents Chick Publications' *The Prophet* (Crusader #17).

Littleton, C. Scott, General Editor. *Mythology: The Illustrated Anthology of World Myth & Storytelling.* San Diego, CA: Thunder Bay Press, 2002. This book details a number of specific myths connected to the various gods and goddesses. It doesn't even try to list them all or do them all justice; it picks and chooses. Still, the book is humongous, yet very easy to read. Much longer descriptions of some myths than available elsewhere. Thoroughly illustrated.

Morey, Robert. *The Islamic Invasion: Confronting the World's Fastest Growing Religion.* Eugene, Oregon: Harvest House Publishers, 1992. This book is an important overview to answer specific questions: 1) What is Islam? 2) Where did it come from? 3) Why is it a threat to the world today? It includes sections on the Muslims' holy books, the *Qur'an* and the multi-volume *Hadith.* It also has a photographic section on Allah as a moon god. Illustrated.

Overy, Richard, editor. *The Times Complete History of the World.* New York: Times Books (Harper Collins), 6th edition, 2004. This is a book of maps that step the reader through history, with explanatory text. Thoroughly illustrated.

Parrinder, Geoffrey. *A Dictionary of Non-Christian Religions.* Philadelphia: Westminster Press, 1971. Parrinder (1910-2005) was one of the top authorities on world religions and Professor of the Comparative Study of Religions at King's College, London from 1958-77 and the author of over 30 books. He spent almost two decades as a missionary in Benin and the Ivory Coast. I have used this dictionary for 20 years. It was one of the few sources available in the 1970s-90s about non-Christian religions. Emphasis on Hinduism, Buddhism and Islam. As with all books, it cannot possibly list *all* the deities. Illustrated.

Porada, Edith (with collaboration of RH Dyson & contributions by CK Wilkinson). *The Art of Ancient Iran, Pre-Islamic Cultures.* New York: Crown Publishers, Inc. Art of the World, 1962. Porada (1912-1994) was Arthur Lehman Professor Emeritus of Art History and Archaeology at Columbia University and the world's leading authority on ancient cylinder seals. This book, following her many travels, is considered the standard introduction to the field of Iranian art history. Illustrated, largely with color photographs. (In my copy they are physically inserted into the text.)

Roaf, Michael. *Cultural Atlas of Mesopotamia & the Ancient Near East.* Oxfordshire, England: Andromeda Oxford Limited, 1990. Using 53 maps as a starting point, Roaf added 468 illustrations (most in color) to show the history, culture and everyday life of citizens in 20 specific sites, and in Mesopotamia in general. Very well-compiled special features, as well as a comprehensive index.

Schnoebelen, William. *Wicca: Satan's Little White Lie.* Ontario, California: Chick Publications, 1990. If you want to hear about Wicca and its true Satanic origin by a former Wiccan and Satanist, then this is the book for you. See some of the references to Schnoebelen's book in the Index and see for yourself. We are happy to have it available at Chick Publications.

Sharkey, Don. *The Woman Shall Conquer.* Libertyville, Illinois: Prow Books/ Franciscan Marytown Press, 1954, 1973 & 1976. This book claims to have "all the recent, authenticated apparitions of our Lady since 1830" that "point to the great day of *her* ultimate triumph over the forces of Satan." (From the back cover, emphasis mine.) This is a thoroughly Catholic, Mary-worshipping book.

Tetlow, Jim, Oakland, Roger & Myers, Brad. *Queen of Rome, Queen of Islam, Queen of All: The Marian Apparition's Plan to Unite All Religions under the Roman Catholic Church.* New York: Eternal Productions, 2006. This book is an amazing exposé of Satan's plan for the Roman Catholic "Mary" as the all-encompassing "goddess" who will unite all religions in the End of time.

Tomkins, Peter. *The Magic of Obelisks.* New York: Harper & Row, 1981. This book contains more information about obelisks, their origin, significance and the occultic rites connected with them than any other book I have ever seen. It also relates that Nero killed Christians by the obelisk on Vaticanus hill. On the other hand, it is in no way Christian; and it discusses many things about filthy occultic rituals and beliefs most people would rather not know.

Turner, Patricia & Coulter, Charles Russell. *Dictionary of Ancient Deities.* New York: Oxford University Press, 2000. This is no minor dictionary. The back cover claims it is "the most comprehensive reference ever compiled on ancient deities from every tradition." And I agree. While it doesn't cover *every* god and goddess I have ever found (see p. 91 of this book for the reason why), it covers *most* of them, in a fair and evenhanded manner. If you are researching about ancient deities, this book is an absolute must. The index is one of the best I have ever seen, and quickly points you to the information you are seeking.

Whyte-Melville, G. J. *Sarchedon: A Legend of the Great Queen.* London: Ward, Lock & Co., Limited, 1871. This is a novel set in the days of Queen Semiramis—but as if she had lived many centuries after the true wife of Nimrod actually lived. It is dedicated to Austin Layard, discoverer of the ancient Assyrian Library of Ashurbanipal. So in many ways, it attempts to be a "historical novel." It bases itself upon the discoveries of ancient writings in Babylonia, Sumer to the south and Assyria to the north. It was written in the early days of modern archaeology. However many shortcomings it may have, its description of Semiramis is so well-written that I had to put it in this book.

Wilkinson, Sir John Gardner. *A Popular Account of the Ancient Egyptians, Revised and Abridged from His Larger Work.* New York: Crescent Books, 1988. A facsimile copy of the two-volume work first published by John Murray, made into one volume. Originally published in 1836. Abridged and other matter added in 1853. Wilkinson is the "father of British Egyptology," who recorded information otherwise lost in later years due to looting, decay and vandalism of ancient sites. Excellent woodcuts of all kinds of Egyptian life, as found in drawings and carvings he found personally during his journeys.

Wilkinson, Philip & Philip, Neil, Consultant. *DK Illustrated Dictionary of Mythology: Heroes, Heroines, Gods & Goddesses from Around the World.* London: Dorling Kindersley Limited, 1998. This book is small, but it is packed with information. There are numerous color photos on every page, small but tightly-written summaries of each deity, and the whole is grouped under the different continents of the world. Thoroughly illustrated.

ELECTRONIC MEDIA

Ages Software. Available at www.ageslibrary.com. Sources used for this book include:
- **Master Christian Library**
- **Reformation Library**
- **Jacob Neusner, translator.** *Babylonian Talmud: Translation & Commentary*

SwordSearcher Software. Available at www.swordsearcher.com. See the website for more information about books and study tools. A quick-to-learn and amazing program.